SKIN and SCUBA DIVING

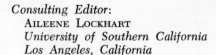

PHYSICAL EDUCATION ACTIVITIES SERIES

Consulting Editor:
AILEENE LOCKHART
University of Southern California
Los Angeles, California

Evaluation Materials Editor:
JANE A. MOTT
Smith College
Northampton, Massachusetts

ARCHERY, Wayne C. McKinney
BADMINTON, Margaret Varner Bloss
BADMINTON, ADVANCED, Wynn Rogers
BASKETBALL FOR MEN, Glenn Wilkes
BASKETBALL FOR WOMEN, Frances Schaafsma
BIOPHYSICAL VALUES OF MUSCULAR ACTIVITY, E. C. Davis,
    Gene A. Logan, and Wayne C. McKinney
BOWLING, Joan Martin
CANOEING AND SAILING, Linda Vaughn and Richard Stratton
CIRCUIT TRAINING, Robert P. Sorani
CONDITIONING AND BASIC MOVEMENT CONCEPTS, Jane A. Mott
CONTEMPORARY SQUARE DANCE, Patricia A. Phillips
FENCING, Muriel Bower and Torao Mori
FIELD HOCKEY, Anne Delano
FIGURE SKATING, Marion Proctor
FOLK DANCE, Lois Ellfeldt
GOLF, Virginia L. Nance and E. C. Davis
GYMNASTICS FOR MEN, A. Bruce Frederick
GYMNASTICS FOR WOMEN, A. Bruce Frederick
HANDBALL, Michael Yessis
ICE HOCKEY, Don Hayes
JUDO, Daeshik Kim
KARATE AND PERSONAL DEFENSE, Daeshik Kim and Tom Leland
LACROSSE FOR GIRLS AND WOMEN, Anne Delano
MODERN DANCE, Esther E. Pease
PADDLEBALL, Philip E. Allsen and Alan Witbeck
PHYSICAL AND PHYSIOLOGICAL CONDITIONING FOR MEN, Benjamin Ricci
RUGBY, J. Gavin Reid
SKIING, Clayne Jensen and Karl Tucker
SKIN AND SCUBA DIVING, Albert A. Tillman
SOCCER, Richard L. Nelson
SOCCER AND SPEEDBALL FOR WOMEN, Jane A. Mott
SOCIAL DANCE, William F. Pillich
SOFTBALL, Marian E. Kneer and Charles L. McCord
SQUASH RACQUETS, Margaret Varner Bloss and Norman Bramall
SWIMMING, Betty J. Vickers and William J. Vincent
SWIMMING, ADVANCED, James A. Gaughran
TABLE TENNIS, Margaret Varner Bloss and J. R. Harrison
TAP DANCE, Barbara Nash
TENNIS, Joan Johnson and Paul Xanthos
TENNIS, ADVANCED, Chet Murphy
TRACK AND FIELD, Kenneth E. Foreman and Virginia L. Husted
TRAMPOLINING, Jeff T. Hennessy
VOLLEYBALL, Glen H. Egstrom and Frances Schaafsma
WEIGHT TRAINING, Philip J. Rasch
WRESTLING, Arnold Umbach and Warren R. Johnson

PHYSICAL EDUCATION

ACTIVITIES SERIES

WITHDRAWN SKIN
and SCUBA
DIVING

ALBERT A. TILLMAN

Associate Professor
Department of Physical Education
California State College
Los Angeles, California

WM. C. BROWN COMPANY PUBLISHERS
DUBUQUE, IOWA

Printed in the United States of America

Preface

If there is anything a diver likes better than diving, it's talking about diving. One thing a diver doesn't like to do is to sit and write about diving. The written word has a way of being permanent and anything that is as dynamic and about which there are so many technical controversies as skin and SCUBA diving just can't stand still. What the author has done is to present current information, but he urges you to keep an open mind about diving technology. There is a fantastic world yet to explore and a great deal more to learn.

This booklet includes information for both the beginner and more skilled diver. Emphasis has been placed not only on a consideration of "how" but on the basic "why." Purposeful practice and knowledgeable performance are sought.

Self-evaluation questions are distributed throughout this text. These afford the reader typical examples of the kinds of understandings and levels of skill that he should be acquiring as progress is made toward mastery of diving. The reader should not only answer the printed questions but should pose additional ones as a self-check on learning. In some instances the reader may find that he cannot respond fully and accurately to a question until all the material has been studied extensively or more actual experience has been gained. From time to time the reader should return to these and other troublesome questions until he has truly mastered the answers or developed the skills called for, as the case may be.

Contents

SKIN and SCUBA DIVING

What Is Diving Like?

If you haven't had the urge to go under water as yet then you're a rarity among the peoples of this planet. A liquid jungle covering three-fourths of our world beckons us to return to a place where our primordial ancestors once swam before they eventually moved to the land.

And why shouldn't you want to return! Your very own circulatory system courses with the rhythm and chemistry of the sea. They now say the dolphin may be the first of land creatures to have returned to the underwater world of the oceans. Will you, Man, follow?

There are a great number of reasons for going under water and they will increase in future years. Probably the most motivating force behind most participation is the anticipation of exploring a strange and mysterious place. You will find that exploration and discovery are th ebasic excitements of Skin and SCUBA diving.

But there is much more to it. You will find the physical satisfaction of free flight, of movement without the restrictions of gravity, of being close to the experience that Leonardo Da Vinci hoped for in his wild sketches of man flying in air and water. Once you are trained and experienced, slipping through the surface into a lovely and tranquil bit of liquid wilderness will be effortless and fulfilling of the need to escape the routine bustle of your everyday existence.

Many people find the physical experience and perhaps the exploring challenge enough to sustain their attraction to the sport for many years of diving. But the true veteran enthusiasts move down and outward on the tree of diving interests. The hunter, the artist, the scientist, the photographer, and the archaeologist eventually see in diving a tool for pursuing a technical interest in places where no man has ever been before.

WHAT IS DIVING LIKE?

The underwater world serves as both playground and laboratory, playing field and classroom, sanctuary and place of challenge. Whether you approach your diving from a recreational or professional standpoint, you will inevitably branch off into several of the exciting special interest areas of diving.

THE HIERARCHY OF INTERESTS

The interest of first magnitude, that from which the heroes of modern diving are being recruited, appears to be underwater photography. Why? Because diving is a hidden sport—there are no wildly cheering or admiring spectators while one is swimming under water. The roar of the crowd has a lot to do with the usual drive to perform and improve skills. Divers must seek appreciation and acknowledgment ex post facto—after they've performed.

Underwater photography provides a concrete, visual record of having seen and conquered. It requires a combination of the most refined skills of diving and the technical artistry of photography. The results supply a permanent record to be admired long after a dive. Best of all, however, the sportsman has not destroyed nor taken from the underwater world, but instead, has recorded a precious moment in time.

Spearfishing, or underwater hunting, is perhaps more physically demanding than all other diving interests. But there is a subhierarchy in spearfishing that recognizes as the pure athlete the diver who skin-dives holding his breath, as opposed to SCUBA diving, where a self-contained underwater breathing appartus, and a nonmechanized type of spear are utilized.

The only legitimate competitive sport aspect of diving that has developed to any degree, spearfishing is by far the most popular diving pursuit in the prime diving areas of the Mediterranean and Australia. Since this competition is based on the killing of life, conservation forces and officials in other sports have not accorded this sport much credit. Whatever the moral values involved, spearfishermen, who take on large game fish in the undersea environment, must be highly skilled and physically sound athletes.

One cannot explore the land of Neptune and not be struck with curiosity. Ever since Roger Bacon answered the question of how many teeth a horse had with the simple response "count them," the discipline of science has been on the upswing. In a like manner the diver through general exposure to unknowns and with native curiosity asks questions and finds answers. The recreational diver easily steps into the role of

2

amateur scientist and is providing data now that may revolutionize our entire body of knowledge of the sea. Take for example the discovery of the rivers of sand off the tip of Baja, California. Divers on expedition there accidentally uncovered and filmed an amazing geological phenomenon —the eroding sands of a continent moving like a river into hundred-foot sand falls dropping into abysmal submarine canyons. Its meaning? Perhaps this may be the answer to the formation of new continents over millions of years. Other divers have captured living fossil fish, creatures who had never been seen other than as impressions in a prehistoric rock.

Divers today are writing new history books. Wrecks and artifacts on the sea floor have yielded new insights into the events and ancient ways of life that have shaped our destinies. While new knowledge is exciting in itself, another breed of diver, the treasure hunters, are tracing the routes of Spanish galleons—mint ships—to their final resting places. Today, silver dubloons are as common as golf balls in the locker rooms of diving.

HOW YOU FEEL UNDER WATER

It is difficult to explain the many-splendored sensations of being under water. Perhaps it is important at this point to differentiate between the act of skin-diving and that of SCUBA diving. The words themselves are not as descriptive as they should be but by common usage they are well established.

Skin diving is most distinctly characterized by the holding of one's breath, a surface breath, during a descent and ascent under water. Generally, such diving is aided only by a pair of swim fins used for propulsion, a glass plated mask for vision, and a snorkel tube for surface relaxation. An individual diver, depending on the temperature and other physical aspects of the diving water, may add a protective rubber suit and a whole host of other accessories.

The SCUBA diver is generally equipped with all of the devices of the skin diver, but rather than depending upon the surface air for each dive, he carries a supply with him from which to partake as needed at various depths.

The entire process of diving, skin and SCUBA, is extremely easy. There are many millions of enthusiasts and by happy accident they manage to engage somewhat successfully in the sport. Driving an automobile or an airplane is no more difficult if one ignores the refinements necessary to cope with the unforeseen and the inherent hazards. A new driver may manage to get out of his driveway but what of his fate on an expressway or when he tries to park on a hill? The new diver encounters similar complexities as he moves from his backyard pool to open water. In the interests of safety, comfort, and satisfaction, he should be well prepared in knowledge and skill concerning such diverse subjects as physics, oceanography, physiology, marine biology, equipment and watermanship.

But how does it feel when you finally arrive at that point of readiness with the right knowledge, skill, frame of mind, and equipment? Although the experience will depend to an extent upon the temperature and clarity of the water, you should feel the young Turk's fire, that driving force of adventure. You'll be amazed when you open your eyes, and are able to see with looking-glass clarity a panorama of wonderful things that formerly were only pictures in a magazine. You will find, by concentrating on your breathing, that you can sink or rise at will with complete relaxation. When you are ready to move through the water, you will find a real sense of physical power as you push the fin, an extension on your feet, against the water. Creatures below move casually out of your way as you glide almost effortlessly down to sit on a living coral reef, there to look in awe at a gigantic natural kaleidoscopic scene that until that moment could have been touched by only the hand of God.

You'll not want to return to the world above. I guarantee this. But you'll be forced to. Your air supply is limited and there are physiological laws that must be heeded. Besides, you'll want to tell someone about the experience! You may even wish you had a picture or could capture one of the exotic fish, or pluck a souvenir piece of coral. You'll get around to all of these things in time but first you'll run into a number of physical and environmental problems that will demand your knowledge and very best skill in diving. Well, these things this booklet proposes to give you.

2

Skills Essential
for Everyone

There is no substitute for good watermanship in any kind of aquatics activity. Skin and SCUBA diving which take you into remote and uncontrolled waters require even more extensive and demanding water skills.

Watermanship can be explained broadly as your total ability to propel and maintain yourself with ease in the water environment. A basic pattern of muscular coordination, kinesthetic sense, and confidence generally is reflected in your degree of watermanship.

You may be led to think of watermanship as another way of saying swimming ability but this would be somewhat like saying that running is the essential physical skill in sports involving the legs. It plays only a contributing role. You as a diver face two other challenges that require unique skills: the equipment and the environment.

There has been·a tendency to assume that the donning of this equipment magically creates diving ability. This is no more than saying a gun in hand makes a hunter. The equipment is basically designed to aid you and your personal skills in coping with a dense, wet, foreign environment that tends to be unpredictable and prevents your natural breathing. But in the process of aiding one's personal adaptations to the underwater world, the equipment tends to complicate participation and forces one to develop new and additional skills.

THE BASIC PERSONAL SKILLS

In the development of diving, skin diving came first because you are capable of doing this with the bare minimum of paraphenalia, namely a bubble of air between your eyes and the water. Skin diving today, however, has taken a back seat to the increasingly popular act of diving with

After jumping into the water, can you immediately position your-self on the surface for adjust-ments?

While wearing SCUBA?

With fins in hand?

Evaluation Questions

SCUBA (self contained underwater breathing apparatus). In fact, the current generation of divers condescendingly tends to describe the pure act of holding one's breath while diving (skin diving) as "bottom scratching without a bubble machine."

Clearing the Mask—Whichever camp you choose to join in this friendly "war" between enthusiasts, the use of a *face mask* to provide the vital bubble of air *for visual purposes* is universally necessary. An elaborately outfitted expedition to the Great Barrier Reef of Australia would be incomplete without the diminutive mask in every kit.

The naked human eye, which is almost blind under water, can see clearly if an air space is placed between it and the water. When wearing the face mask, objects under water appear closer and about 25 per cent larger. The first efforts by divers to create air pockets was to use goggles, however there were several drawbacks to these. The two lenses caused a great amount of water to enter the nose, causing infection of the sinus in some cases, and there was no way to equalize the pressure in the goggles.

The device which followed the goggles was the face plate (or face mask). The mask that is most commonly in use today is the type that completely covers the nose and the eyes, but not the mouth. This diving mask is made of rubber walls in the shape of a very short cylinder. The mask has a sealed glass covering at one end, and the rubber is shaped to form a watertight seal on the diver's face at the opposite end. This type of mask not only keeps water out of the nose but allows the diver to equalize pressure by exhaling out of the nose into the mask. Because there is only one plate of glass, there is no great amount of visual distortion.

Evaluation Questions

Can you clear your mask once as you hold your breath while skin diving?

Twice on one breath?

Three times?

In using the face mask, a basic personal skill required. You must learn to fit the proper mask to your face and maintain the bubble of air captured therein. The loss of the bubble (it goes to the surface without you) means it must be replaced from an air supply such as; (1) the surface; (2) the lungs, if skin diving; or (3) the air tank, if SCUBA diving. Whether skin or SCUBA diving, the air must be passed to the mask through the nose. This new supply of air replaces the water which has replaced the escaped air bubble in your mask.

The skill comes in the ability to substitute the air for the water gently without allowing any of this new air to escape the mask. There are several techniques. You cautiously lift a small portion of the edge of the mask right beneath the nose, blow out gently and continuously, then replace, sealing the mask to the face after all the water has been removed (highly skilled divers are fictitiously expected to find dust in the mask after performing this clearing process).

Manufacturers have "automated" some of the more recent masks with pig snout valves so that a simple snort effects the clearing process. The clearing skill is not made obsolete by this innovation as the unsnouted mask is still abundantly in the majority.

Entry Methods—Now that you can see under water, you'd better learn how to get in. Nothing starts a dive off on a sour note more emphatically than a clumsy beginning. Fortunately, many diving situations are refined by the presence of a pool or boat ladder and a diver is provided, to some degree, a gripping rail by which to enter and exit. But the ladder doesn't insure a graceful performance; on the contrary, great care should be taken to remember to remove swim fins from feet and objects from hands when attempting to use a ladder. Like most aids, the ladder requires its own set of techniques and adds its own inherent hazards.

Divers with a flair for theatrics and wishing to avoid contact with potentially entangling ladders, jump in. Sound simple? It's not when you're encased in dozens of straps, a rubber suit, dangling various accessory devices, and carrying about fifty pounds of dead weight while out of the water. The jump actually becomes a well-coordinated fall.

The most universal method of entry is what has been called the "lifesaving entry" but divers usually refer to it as the *Giant Stride*. The process of execution is:

1. Step off the side of pool, dock, or boat (recommended no higher than three feet) in a wide stride fashion.
2. Place the palm of the hand over the glass part of the face mask and grip it firmly to the face to prevent its unseating.
3. Slap the water with the other hand if it is free, and after entering, bring the fins together vigorously as in the scissors kick.
4. *Caution!* Immediately look at your entry spot before entry so that you will not jump onto another diver.
5. While in mid-air fix your vision off your entry spot to an area 50 feet in front of you in order to maintain proper entry form.
6. If you are carrying objects in your hand, they should be held to the side so that the force of entry will not drive them into your mask or head.
7. This entry usually will prevent a diver from penetrating down into the water, and position him immediately at the surface where he can readjust his equipment and check on his buddy.

Other acceptable entries include the *front roll* to which all the preceding safety precautions also apply. This is achieved by tucking the head, leaning forward, and rolling into the water. Hesitant beginners can build up to a standing roll by starting from a kneeling position.

Feet together is preferred for a streamlined entry from higher entry areas where the preceding entries would involve too much impact to vital areas. Streamline the penetration (which will take you a few feet below the surface, depending upon the height) by pointing the tips of your fins downward during the plunge.

Well, there you are in the water but you're not under. This requires another basic skill, that of getting under water. You can include this skill with the general process referred to in diving as "descending" and "ascending."

Evaluation Questions

Can you sink feet first, bend, and swim off without breaking the surface with the feet?

Can you sink feet first to the bottom of the deep pool area by controlling the volume of air in your lungs?

Surface Diving—The act of getting under water can be a very important one to skin divers. This is true when you consider that a poor surface dive (getting under) expends strength and energy before your underwater exposure even begins. A poorly executed surface dive results in surface thrashing which scares desirable sea life but can attract the larger animals with vicious propensities.

The *jackknife surface* dive is the most commonly used by divers since it gives the diver a sort of push off start from the surface. It is easily performed from a stationary float or a swimming stroke. Here is the procedure:

1. Reach downward in the water as if to touch your toes.
2. Allow your hips to hinge your body forward; this draws your legs toward the surface.
3. Allow your legs to break surface; hold together with fins pointed back, and let them rise smoothly out of the water. Correct form allows the fins to follow the hips in an arch back under water.

The higher the legs come out of the water, the more weight will be exerted and this will drive the diver downward. No kicking is necessary until you are completely submerged.

The *feet first* method is a quiet, relaxed surface dive. In its simplest form, a diver merely lays his arms to his sides, with his body in a straight line under him, and allows his head to sink beneath the surface. When completely submerged, the diver jackknifes and swims off.

This method can be varied and accentuated by lifting one's arms overhead so that their weight helps drive the diver under. A strong leg scissors kick will push more of the diver out of the water, causing a greater weight to be exerted downward when completed.

Surfacing—Surfacing upon ascent from a dive can be hazardous if proper technique is not developed. One effective course of action is to come up with one hand raised, pointed at the area of surfacing. This prevents head contact with floating objects on the surface. Look up as ascent is made and endeavor to spiral as you come so that there is a 360° coverage. Observance should be made of the area that surrounds the diver and an occasional downward look will prevent any creatures from closing in without noticing them.

When surfacing into kelp or a similar entanglement, both hands over the head will allow a penetration and spreading of the material so the head can be pushed through.

Underwater Swimming—Another skill you'll need and one that most barefooted swimmers find difficulty in achieving is the art of movement under water. Divers wearing fins can usually master this skill quickly since they have tremendous additional power to push against the resistance of the water bulk.

A diver in the unpredictable restrictions and temperatures of the open water has a grave responsibility to conserve his strength and energy in every way possible. Perfecting the underwater swimming ability even though the "fins seem to do the work" can conserve a great amount of basic human resources for any unforeseen emergency.

Very few submarines have appendages to grasp and pull them through the water. The idea is to streamline the front and push from the rear. This requires power in the rear. The barefooted swimmer, therefore, may have to add arm power to compensate for lack of rear leg power. A fin-footed diver should have the power if he uses a thrusting bicycle-type kick. Although much controversy still rages about the aqua-dynamics of the fin, the push backwards against the water provides the source of power.

Veteran divers smooth out the bicycling-type kick into a smoother flutter-type kick, the energy generating from the hip accentuated by "loose knees and ankles" which allow the fins to break apart to a gap of about 14 inches.

(The flutter-type kick is also suitable for surface swimming with fins. Keep the kick low in the water to avoid splashing because some contend surface disturbance attracts predatory large fish, e.g., sharks.)

The arms should be laid against the sides of the body (hands may be used to fin a little) unless spear guns or other equipment is being extended in front of diver. If vision ahead is restricted, if the water is dirty, or if the diver is watching the bottom as he goes, a hand should be extended in front of the head to contact rocks, other hazardous projections, or the walls of the pool.

Breath Holding and Hyperventilation—Breath holding and hyperventilation are more directly skills of skin diving but the SCUBA diver out of air must return to the natural way at various times throughout his diving. You will want to have the confidence in SCUBA diving of knowing that you are not a slave to the breathing unit and can switch over to a skin diving role without undue distress.

It's not uncommon to see groups of people standing around with puffed cheeks and discolored faces. People have always wondered how long they could hold their breaths. Divers now have a functional reason for so testing themselves and it is important to find one's breaking point. There's a certain confidence born of the knowledge that with special training and technique the breath can be held by most physically fit individuals for about a minute and thirty seconds. In that period of time, a man can shave completely, climb the stairs in a six-story building, or build a fire in the fireplace. A diver can untangle a fouled propeller, spear several fish and string them, or on a shallow dive explore about 450 square feet of underwater area. The point is that it can be done if *necessary*—not that it *should* be done.

There is significant evidence that breath holding can create cardiac abnormalities. There is much that needs explaining through scientific research on this topic. With this message of caution, the ways to improve the skill of breath holding are now described.

How unusually big a breath should you take before a dive? This is a good question but not easily answered. The common tendency is to take an unusually large gulp of air which, while discomforting on the surface, is relieved by the pressure progressively in accordance with the depth one dives. This does allow for better equalization of all air spaces, provides more oxygen, and gives more space for carbon dioxide. The disadvantage of a large breath is in connection with the maximum buoyancy achieved. The diver finds himself fighting to get down the first few feet of descent. This expends energy, uses up oxygen, and builds up carbon dioxide rapidly at the start of the dive.

Some divers have met the buoyancy problem of a maximum breath by wearing a weight belt. While this eases the diver past the first-few-

Can you swim under water holding your breath for one length of the pool?

Two lengths? Three?

Evaluation Questions

feet-of-descent struggle, it creates an added burden upon the ascent. It becomes of questionable value when one analyzes the compression of a skin diver at 33 feet. At that depth, most divers have been squeezed to a point of negative buoyancy and weights would accentuate the difficulty.

Perhaps the more desirable type of breath to take would be what is called a "half breath" which in reality is what would be a normal inhalation of a person involved in moderate activity. Once again we are dealing with relative values; however, a good general principle is to avoid any type of weighting devices in skin diving unless a compensating type of inflatable device is used in conjunction.

How can the actual breath-holding time be increased? There are a number of basic techniques, some scientific and some in the realm of folklore. Here is a variety:

1. Improve physical condition in general and breath-holding time will increase correspondingly.
2. Do deep breathing exercises daily to improve ventilating capacity and enlarge the thoracic cavity.
3. "Fool" the breathing mechanism by swallowing. This seems to be basically psychological although there may be some sort of physical tension released by the action.
4. "Psych" oneself by setting the mind on something other than the need to breathe, e.g., counting tile squares on the bottom of the pool. This occasionally happens automatically in diving when one becomes extremely interested in something found on the bottom.
5. Learn to hyperventilate by forced breathing. Breathe deeply, with the emphasis on exhalation. This purges the breathing stimulant, carbon

Evaluation Questions

Can you equalize the pressure on your ears by pinching your nose and blowing?

By pushing the mask against the face?

By swallowing? By yawning?

dioxide, out of the respiratory system and to a minor degree "beefs up" the percentage of oxygen in the lungs. (Although there is approximately 20 per cent oxygen in the air we breathe, normal breathing utilizes only about one-fourth of that percentage. The remaining three-fourths is exhaled.) There is not a set number of deep breath cycles; however, about five or six seem to be reasonably safe for most individuals. Experienced divers may do such deep breathing for forty or more repetitions but there is great danger involved. Any irregularity in body chemistry can result in serious malfunction leading to unconsciousness.

Hyperventilation can and should be practiced so that you know your personal reaction to the process and to establish your ultimate breaking point in case of emergencies involving prolonged submersion, e.g., swimming under burning oil. *There should be careful supervision of all such efforts.*

This general discourse on breath holding (known technically as "voluntary apnea") might be summarized by saying that a good skin diver without any special techniques does not breathe for a period of 30 to 45 seconds—this means a skilled diver employing no unnecessary movements while under water. Depth itself permits one to prolong breath holding and hyperventilation can be employed in moderation to add to this.

Remember! Any deviation from normal breathing of normal atmospheric air creates potential additional hazard. This is true also of any psychological manipulation the diver may inspire within himself.

Equalization Methods—Equalizing pressure is another basic skill of the competent diver. The "diver's squeeze" is probably the most harrassing of all the skin diver's problems. If he cannot equalize his internal air cavities to the pressure of the outside water, there will be discomfort or pain.

Discomfort is a more desirable warning sign than pain for it is the result of sensing unequalization in the first stages. The diver who fails to heed such signs is inviting serious trouble.

The most common need of the diver is to "clear the ears." This is necessary because the air space known as the eustachian tube lying internally behind the eardrum (tympanic membrane) has not received sufficient air flow from the intake breath to compensate for the squeezing outside water pressure. This is usually the result of the eustachian tube's being closed by tissue growth or mucus where it connects to the throat. Some divers can never completely open this air passage until they have been specially treated by a doctor. Slight mucus formation (sticky eustachian tube) can be overcome by pinching the nose or holding the mask skirt against the nostrils and gently blowing outward several times. Success is felt when there is a "click" on each side and a fullness is felt behind each eardrum.

Other techniques for "clearing" that are sometimes successful are swallowing, moving the jaws, holding the mask tight to the face and blowing, rolling the head from side to side, and ascending a few feet. Sometimes it is necessary to surface, remove the mask and hold the nose, and repeatedly but gently blow the nose.

Veteran divers insure against ear squeeze by starting the held-nose-blowing routine upon arising on the day of a dive and continuing it on the way there, while putting equipment on, and all of the time they are in the water. The tissue involved in the eustacian tube can be exercised, toned, and its response to equalization improved by practice.

3

Better Divers
Master These Skills

Everyone wants to look and behave like a "pro." To be one, however, doesn't just happen; it requires continued learning and improvement. In diving, most of the advanced skills are involved with the use of SCUBA and then with special interest area application. Here are some skills to try and to perfect if you want the champion image.

SURFACE SWIMMING AND LIFESAVING

1. Don't thrash water with your kick. Lower your kick in the water by accentuating the bicycling action in the flutter kick.
2. Use the snorkel so your head can stay face down and maintain a straight line.
3. Don't forget to look up occasionally in order to get your bearings, check on your buddy, and avoid obstacles.
4. Learn to swim on your back so you can use this as a rest stroke for your swim back from a dive.
5. Don't be ashamed to maintain a leisurely pace. Many beginning divers exhaust themselves getting to a diving area by swimming in a sort of race with their buddies or other divers. Speed swimming doesn't allow you to surface-explore the bottom thoroughly on the way out.
6. Don't try to push a float with sacks and gear hanging from it. Arrange everything so all will ride high and be supported by the float.

WEIGHTING

The SCUBA unit will probably add several pounds of negative buoyancy to a dive when the cylinder is full. A diver should reweight to compensate for the addition of the unit. The tank will become more bouyant

Which items the diver is wearing
affect his buoyancy?

How does depth affect buoyancy?

How can a diver compensate for
loss of buoyancy?

Evaluation Questions
BUOYANCY

as the air in it is depleted but a diver should also remember that much of his surface buoyancy is lost by the time he has descended to 33 feet and the loss continues at a lesser rate the deeper a diver goes.

BUDDY BREATHNG

This is an emergency skill involving two divers breathing from one unit. The purpose in learning to do this is to prepare for air depletion, malfunction, or other cases where one diver loses his supply of air.

Side to Side—The diver with the air supply lies on his left side while his buddy faces him. Positioning is maintained by the diver in need by holding on to the upper right arm of the other diver or by holding the tank straps. The mouthpiece can then be passed back and forth between the two, allowing it to bubble freely in transit. (Two hose regulators will free flow if the housing is below the mouthpiece.) Each diver takes two breaths and holds on the second breath. If swimming, forward vision should be maintained as continuously as possible.

Tandem—The diver in need takes a position behind the unit diver, holding his position by the strap. The mouthpiece is passed back over the head of the unit diver to the diver in need who rides on the unit diver's back in tandem fashion.

FREE ASCENT

This is another emergency skill used in reaching the surface when the air supply is no longer available. It merely involves a diver looking up,

Diagram A:

BUOYANCY

swimming up, and exhaling as he goes. The crucial aspect of this skill is to maintain a continuous exhalation (whistle "America") on the ascent, and to make the ascent slowly if expansive pressure is felt in lungs.

Remember! There is usually ample supply of oxygen in the lungs to maintain life and the partial pressure of CO_2 will be relieved so that the impulse to breathe is withheld. The danger is in not exhaling; otherwise the possibility of air embolism is great. Keep exhaling all of the way in a swimming ascent.

This technique can be practiced in a swimming pool by starting in the deep end of the pool and slant ascending to the shallow end. Open water practice can be hazardous and should be extremely well supervised if tried at all. The practicing diver can use a functioning unit as a ready aid in case of difficulty at any time during practice ascent.

There is no need to ditch the unit even though it no longer supplies air. It may refunction in shallower depths, and devoid of compressed air will probably add to a diver's buoyancy.

DITCH AND RECOVERY

An exercise that involves a number of skills, areas of knowledge, and more important a psychological testing is the Ditch and Recovery, often referred to as Don and Doff. It is not a practical skill in itself but merely demonstrates a diver's complete proficiency with SCUBA in one process.

Check your swimming strokes and times under water. Can you flutter kick?

Scissors kick? Frog kick? Dolphin?

With one fin? Without fins?

Evaluation Questions

Ditch—

1. Use seated or kneeling position.
2. Release weight belt and place in balance across the thighs (knees when kneeling).
3. Breathe shallowly at all times to limit buoyancy.
4. Release SCUBA straps and pull SCUBA over head to a position in front of the body, or between the legs when seated.
5. Place the weight belt in balance across the center of the tank.
6. Adjust the straps (SCUBA) for easy recovery.
7. Remove the mask and place it on the right-hand side of the tank.
8. Take a breath and remove the mouthpiece.
9. Place the mouthpiece under the regulator housing.
10. Ascend slowly, watching and pointing to smallest bubbles of exhalation.
    On Surface—
1. Relax and breathe deeply so as to clear CO_2.
2. Think over your exact plan of recovery.
3. Take a half breath and submerge.

Recovery—

1. Descent—approach SCUBA from the regulator end.
2. Disengage the mouthpiece and raise it to allow a free flow of air.
3. Place the mouthpiece in the mouth and exhale sharply.
4. Take a half breath to check the clarity of the air hoses. (If water is encountered, remove the mouthpiece and raise it, stretching the hose

Evaluation Questions

Can you buddy breathe while swimming side by side?

On your back?

With a one hose regulator?

With a two hose regulator?

Without a mask?

to allow air to blow freely; replace in mouth—if no water is encountered, continue to breathe shallowly.

5. If overly buoyant, or if air is flowing too fast, grasp the regulator housing and lower the mouth (and mouthpiece) to the housing.

6. Establish a shallow breathing rhythm and think out the remaining steps.

7. Locate the mask, seat, and clear.

8. If using a seated position, pull the legs forward and slide into place so the unit is between the legs.

9. Remove the weight belt from the tank and place it across the thighs (seated) or knees (kneeling).

10. Raise the tank overhead and settle into position on your back.

11. Adjust and buckle the SCUBA straps.

12. Buckle on the weight belt.

13. Ascend slowly as before.

The skill of lifesaving in the water isn't necessary to the diver personally. No trained and qualified diver plans, however, to dive alone. This means that each diver assumes a certain responsibility for others. From a moral standpoint, divers are equipped and usually in position to aid distressed aquatic enthusiasts, as well as others in trouble.

There are a few hints that can be directly applied to diving.

1. Utilize any available inflatable gear. Blow up anything, including clothes, that the victim is wearing.

2. Get rid of any objects that are weighty.

19

Can you make a free ascent in the deep end of the pool?

Diagonally from deep to shallow end?

From deep to shallow while swimming on your back, and then without fins?

Evaluation Questions

3. Use spear gun, float, or rope to tow conscious victim rather than making personal contact with any victim capable of taking hold.
4. Don't get rid of your face mask, as a victim who slips down and under can sometimes be found only with a viewing device.
5. The snorkel, with a little adjustment of position, allows the diver to swim in a submerged position and still breathe. Many swimmer rescuers fail; they drop victims because they cannot maintain their own faces out of water in order to breathe sufficiently to match the exertion necessary to effect a rescue.

SCUBA SWIMMING

The new diver will find the additions of SCUBA a cumbersome burden to bear on land. He will find some relief when in the water, but it is necessary to learn special techniques to cope with the inherent restriction of the unit.

Veteran divers are finding that back packs, which have replaced to a great degree the harness arrangements on tanks, provide a fairly stable positioning of the unit on the back. There is nothing quite so annoying as a regulator banging on the back of a diver's head or sliding to and fro on his back while he swims.

On the surface, the cylinder should be allowed to settle low in the water so that the water will carry its weight A sno.rkel is required to achieve the most relaxed performance. The leg kick employed while swimming should be a deep bicycle. This pulls the body into a slanted position from the surface and keeps the cylinder under water.

Evaluation Questions

Can you reach back and turn your air off and on while swimming with SCUBA?

Remove mouthpiece and replace it under water?

All these while swimming on your back?

Swimming under water with SCUBA does not require great power in the kick if a diver is merely exploring. An easy flutter therefore can be employed. Veteran divers are utilizing the dolphin kick more and more. A combination of various kicks is probably the most efficient procedure for SCUBA swimming under water.

Clearing SCUBA Hoses—There is the unusual occasion when you may be pushed into the use of an older model two-hose regulator. The older types do not have nonreturn valves near the mouthpiece and even the new ones show up with missing or defective valves. For this reason, there is this skill to learn.

Clear water from flooded hoses by rolling to your left side, rolling until face up, and exhaling all the while. A final vigorous exhalation blast should displace any and all remaining water.

BAIL OUT

The National Association of Underwater Instructors has outlined a "supertest" that goes beyond Ditch and Recovery. Here are the steps.

1. Stand at the edge of the pool with mask, fins, weight belt, and SCUBA cylinder with regulator mounted but air off.
2. Jump in calling "Geronimo." You are entitled to turn on the air as soon as submerged and breathe from the SCUBA unit; however, by that time you will be resting on the fourteen foot bottom (don't forget to equalize as you descend).
3. The job is then to mount all of the equipment upon yourself in correct order.

Can you clear water from your mask while continuing to swim forward at normal rate and using SCUBA?

Take off mask and replace it?

Switch masks with a buddy?

All these while swimming on your back?

Evaluation Questions

4. You then surface and tread water for fifteen minutes without using the snorkel or breathing from the SCUBA. The treading prevents the performer from taking excessive weight down thus eliminating buoyancy problems.

5. "Bail out" measures skills with equipment and psychological adaptation to being under water. *It can be dangerous* for the inexperienced diver and close supervision must be maintained at all times. A few feet of ascent while breath holding can cause expansion of air in body cavities and result in damage.

4

Progress
Can Be Speeded Up

Practicing diving skills under controlled conditions accelerates your progress and leads you to ultimate proficiency. We carry out such practice through a series of experiences we call *incentive exercises*: fun and games. In fact, if there is any true competitive interaction enjoyed by a majority of divers it lies in this stage of the learning process.

Here are some good ones you'll have some fun with.

Mask Scramble (Skin or SCUBA)—Collect the masks of all participants. Have someone who is not competing toss them into the deep water end of the pool. Swimming and diving from the shallow end of the pool, players scramble retrieving a mask and clearing it before surfacing.
   Variations:
1. Have everyone secure his *own* mask.
2. Play the game "musical chairs." The masks (one less mask than there are participants) are repeatedly tossed, eliminating one by one a diver who comes up without a mask.

Buddy Swap (Skin and SCUBA)—You and a buddy go under water and completely exchange all equipment while there. This can be done against time or in direct competition with other teams.

Race for Life—A very successful contest that has great practical implications involves two-man teams making a rescue of a drowning diver utilizing diving gear, a surface float and the technique of mouth-to-mouth resuscitation. The artificial respiration must be administered after surfacing with victim and bringing him all the way to the shore or finish line.

Can you wear SCUBA but not breathe from it while swimming on the surface?

While treading water?

Each of these without fins?

Evaluation Questions

Follow the Leader—Play the old childhood game of letting "it" set the pace and demonstrate the stunts for the rest of the group to follow. Be imaginative if you're the leader, utilizing all the skills you've learned and trying upside down and on the back positions while performing.

Scavenger Hunt—This is a better ocean or lake routine but sometimes a pool yields a collection of objects (plant a few if necessary to add some interest). A prearranged list of objects to hunt for adds more challenge to the experience. A scavenger hunt is a good way to keep the pool bottom clean too!

Underwater Golf Course—The idea here is to set up 18 "holes" on the bottom of the pool or in some other body of water. Each hole involves the diver in a slightly different skill. For example: Hole 1—switch face masks with a mask left at this hole. Hole 2—switch fins. Hole 3—switch snorkels. Hole 4—solve a math problem ($\frac{1}{2} \times \frac{1}{2} = ?$) on a slate. Hole 5—screw a nut onto a bolt. Hole 6—put a nail puzzle together. Hole 7—put a three piece jigsaw puzzle together. Hole 8—string beads or a weight belt. Hole 9—untie a knot. Hole 10—build a box. Hole 11—recover an object with the teeth. Hole 12—exchange tanks. Hole 13—blow up a balloon. Hole 14—drink water from a plastic squeeze bottle. Hole 15—wind a clock (in a plastic bag). Hole 16—write a poem on a slate with a grease pencil. Hole 17—tie a square knot. Hole 18—blow bubbles into plastic buckets until they lift you to the surface. The player wins who can complete the course in the shortest time.

Communications—You start a hand signal message under water down a line of divers. The last man performs the action requested by the message.

Capture the Flag—In this game, similar to a low organized game from the playground, two teams are organized, each one protecting a plastic diver's flag (or an inner tube can be substituted for the flag). Anyone crossing a center line made by stretching a weighted rope can be captured. Prisoners are released by being tagged by a teammate.

Charades—You submerge and attempt to convey the name of a movie, commercial or other such common interest subject by hands, body, or equipment to the rest of the group watching from the surface.

Divers' Tictactoe—Construct a king size tictactoe playing surface on the bottom of the pool with weighted ropes (or set up with plastic chairs). The divers work as two teams, diving in alternate turns to place themselves in squares. The winning team is the one which manages to place three divers in a straight line of squares. If skin diving, it will be necessary for the best breath holders to go first and the later turns to be made after quick, strategic decisions.

Mine Field—Rig a huge field of penny balloons by anchoring them to weights on the bottom. You are required to wear special belts armed with nails, thumbtacks, or pins. The belts can be made of old webbing or even adhesive tape and are worn on shoulders, hips, calves or in combination. You must swim through the mine field without detonating the mines (breaking balloons). You could add to the difficulty by retrieving objects from the bottom while proceeding to the goal.

Easternaut—Divers are forever trying to complicate the "ultimate" skills' test called *Bail Out*. Try handling an egg during the entire process. It'll have to be guarded like a mother hen would guard it and each diver should carry a plastic bag to clean up any mess.

Game Warden—This is similar to low-organized game called *Red light, Green light*. "It" is the Game Warden and uses a red flag and green flag to signal players. Divers swim on the surface toward the warden and must stop and tread water when the red flag is up. Poachers caught moving after the red flag signal must return to the starting point or not swim during the next turn.

Underwater Hockey—The "puck" is a three pound lead weight. The divers attempt to "kick" it to the opponents' goal using finned feet only. Deep water is recommended to test the underwater skills and mobility of the diver-players.

Sharks and Skin Divers—This is an adaptation of *Red Rover*, only "it" is the shark in the center trying to prevent whichever diver he names from reaching the other side of the pool. The shark can have fins and the skin diver only a mask or SCUBA. Vary the equipment to change the challenge. Tagged divers can become additional sharks in order to speed up the game.

Air Station—This exercise places different types of SCUBA units on the bottom of the pool at various locations. You proceed under water to each station where you turn on the air and breathe from each unit. A number of exhalations are required at each station (easily checked from the deck). A race against time can enhance the challenge.

There are infinite numbers of races, relays, and tag games that can be adapted to provide enjoyable practice for the skills of both skin and SCUBA diving. Put those skills to work making a pleasure out of each pool session and progress will take care of itself.

The Tools of Diving

The story of diving as you will see by its history is based to a great extent on the equipment used. Old salts grumble about all the "hardware" necessary today. Indeed, it is an impressive assortment.

There will be no attempt to tell you everything about each item for that deserves a separate book. You will find some items absolutely necessary and the others of a supplemental nature to provide you with a safer, more enjoyable, and successful diving experience.

If possible do try out equipment before buying it. The next best thing is to watch and talk to instructors or experienced divers. Body types and personal likes create diversities that mean, however, you will eventually have to decide for yourself. The fit is the most important aspect in guiding you. Necessary for you to perform the act of skin diving safely are the following:

Mask	Diver's flag
Snorkel	Knife
Surface float	Personal emergency float (life vest)

Supplemental for you to collect, hunt, record, and stay comfortable are the following:

What is the capacity of the standard cylinder in the diagram?

With what and how is it filled?

What controls the flow of air from the cylinder?

How is it tested and by whom?

Evaluation Questions
STANDARD CYLINDER

Protective suit   Watch
Weights   Compass
Spear gun   Packs for equipment
Gloves   Weight belt
Depth gauge

The mask should be soft to the face but rigid enough to withstand the water pressure. It should have safety glass and its rubber should be protected by rinsing it in fresh water after use and by storing it in the shade.

Swim fins will help you to "fly" under water and allow the free use of your hands for other tasks. The full fin is preferred over the strap fin as it usually provides a snug, custom fit. The rigid, heavy fin takes more power but less strokes; the flexible ones take less power and more strokes.

The *snorkel* should be a simple "J" shape without any tricky valve devices and definitely not built in to the mask. Its easy removal and simple design make it a valuable aid for resting at the surface without entanglement. The *protective* suit comes as a *wet type* which provides insulation but does not restrict movement and the *dry type* which seals out water, provides insulation through dry under-garments, but is somewhat restrictive to movement. There is no doubt that you may find the suit a necessary item in cold water. If so, the *weight belt* also becomes a necessity for the suit adds buoyancy that must be counteracted.

Diagram B:
STANDARD CYLINDER

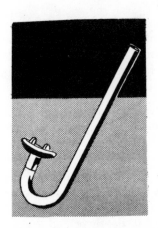

Necessary for you to go SCUBA diving are the same items recommended for skin diving plus the following:

Open circuit SCUBA regulator

The tank or cylinder

Watch
Depth gauge
Compass

The *regulator* should be a time-tested brand but your choice between a one hose or two hose type must be your own. The regulator is a mechanism for metering air without wasting it and unless you are going to become a professional repairman, you need not learn the complexities of its design. It is valuable for you to know its basic principle: simply that air must be supplied and reduced to the pressure and volume dictated by your lungs during a SCUBA dive. It's an automatic faucet that is controlled by (1) your breathing and (2) the surrounding water.

The tank must be certified by an ICC inscription which tells when it was last tested (the man who fills it will tell you when it is time for a new test), and the standard single used will contain approximately 17.2 cubic

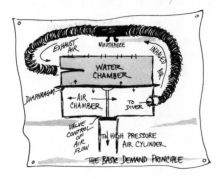

How does the SCUBA regulator function and where is the path of the air from container to exhalation?

What steps would you take under water if the flow of air stopped?

feet of air which under ordinary circumstances won't get you into decompression worries on a dive. Usually the tanks are filled with about 2,000 pounds of air per square inch of pressure. More PSI is possible but the possibility of the development of metal fatigue prompts us to stay with a margin of safety.

The valve at the mouth of the tank regulates, by manual control, the flow of air. The opening to the regulator is sealed over the opening in this valve. When the tank is turned on, the regulator takes over the control of the air. Safety dictates some type of reserve air supply to help you get out of difficulties down below. Some tanks and some regulators have special manually operated devices which hold back a small supply of air until needed and called for by the process of taking it "off reserve."

The assembled SCUBA unit must be attached to the diver and various harnesses and packs are available to take care of this. Once again, selection is dictated by fit and comfort.

The *depth gauge* and *watch* become extremely important to you in SCUBA diving so you can calculate and stay within no-decompression diving.

6

The Technology of Diving

Diving is a labyrinth of technical knowledge. It is entirely possible to participate without understanding the various technologies of the field but your superior performance will result only from a basic foundation in oceanology, physics, and physiology.

OCEANOLOGY

This word denotes a body of learning that describes the sea and its inhabitants. The following things should be known about it:

1. Your planet has water covering three-fourths of its surface.
2. Bacteria are prevalent in all natural water areas and intensified in areas where the wastes of civilization are discarded.
3. Waters of the sea are in a constant state of movement resulting in currents, surface waves, and tides which provide the unpredictable elements which interfere with your planned dive.
4. You should not attempt to swim against a current for even the mildest is exhausting. Plan for currents and endeavor to plot your dive so that they will aid you in returning to home base when you are tired. Rip currents, usually referring to water moving swiftly from shore back to sea, are escaped by swimming diagonally out the side.
5. Tides determine water conditions. Low tides tend to sweep matter out to diving areas, causing dirty water. Great differences between flood and ebb tides usually mean rough water.
6. Cold water is one of your greatest enemies in diving. It can produce fatigue, cramps, mental and physical impairment, and insensibility

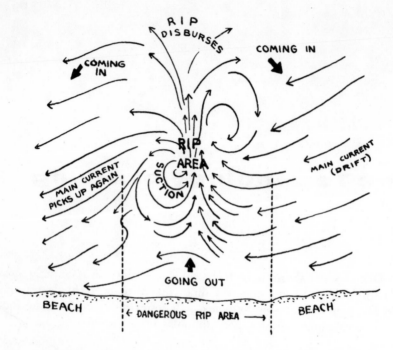

to pain. You will soon discover the phenomenon of the thermocline as you dive increasingly deeper. This is a diving line between layers of water of varying temperatures. It is a rude shock when your arm is extended beyond a thermocline; very much like reaching into the freezer on a hot day.

The Creatures—You should prepare for meeting strange creatures in the depths. There should be no fear involved in this preparation but

merely a sincere respect and alertness. The awesome hazards of land civilization far overshadow those of the underwater frontier.

If there is a general rule about facing the underwater creatures, it probably is *be respectful*. They were there first and many of them have a pride of ownership about a certain piece of bottom that leads them to protect it. You can expect a definite reaction when you poke, annoy, or injure a creature. Merely seeing a diver will seldom cause the animals to bother him.

Take *sharks* for example. They certainly do have teeth and are powerful swimmers but they exist by the millions and rarely bother a diver. Like people, however, sharks are unpredictable from one area to another, from one species to another, and even from one individual shark to another. They can smell, see, hear, feel and bite, but so can bears that frequent the camping areas in our mountains.

Killer whales, the true monsters of the sea, grow up to 30 feet in length. They are fast, have excellent hearing and razor-edged teeth. Waters

they inhabit should be left immediately. *Sea lions* and *seals* are the dogs of the sea and their friendliness or lack of it depends on the mating season or whether you're carrying fish that they feel belong to them.

The moray eel looks as if he were cast for monster films but despite his needle teeth and powerful snake-like body, his behavior is purely defensive and it usually takes considerable poking to arouse his ire. Once again in different areas various species develop more aggressive behavior.

Sting rays, which frequent sandy bottoms everywhere, cause serious difficulty only where you must wade through shallow water to get to a diving area. They sport a serrated stinger at the base of a rat-like tail and its wound is extremely painful. First aid is to remove stinger if in wound, soak wound in hot water to relieve pain, and elevate the limb. See a doctor as soon as possible.

Barracuda are pests in many of the tropical areas but despite their ferocious appearance should cause you little concern. An aggressive movement towards them will usually chase them off. They are attracted to shiny objects.

Jellyfish, which are umbrella-shaped creatures, are more common in the summer season. They are capable of inflicting stings over a wide area of the body. The underside and tentacles contain the stinging fluid. When the diver comes in contact with the underside of the jellyfish the fluid is rubbed off onto the body.

33

The degree of severity of the sting depends upon the skin of the diver. It was found that persons with light, dry skin were affected the most. The first treatment for such a sting is to rub wet sand over the area affected. This removes the stinging fluid from the skin. The stings vary from a slight red area to large welts and are accompanied by a burning sensation. When diving in an area where jellyfish are numerous, it is wise to rub baby oil, heavy mineral oil, or a similar substance on the body. This will protect the skin from the stinging fluid. Always look up and watch for them while surfacing.

The Portuguese man-o-war is in this family. It is very poisonous and its sting can result in death. It is big and slow moving. Care should be taken by a diver when entering temperate waters.

Growths (coral, barnacles, etc.)—Barnacles, worm tubes, corals, and other such growths are very sharp and cause razor-like cuts, almost unnoticed while in the water. The bacterial slime covering these growths and that prevalent in the water makes such wounds slow healing and highly susceptible to infections. Clean such wounds with soap and water and apply an antiseptic.

Sea urchins usually are found in rocky areas. They look like a pin cushion and the spines are brittle and sharp. Stepping on or bumping

into them leaves pieces of the spines embedded under the skin. These are painful and can cause infection.

Some divers claim the spines of sea urchins will eventually dissolve; others, however, complain of aggravating lumps many months after such injury. To avoid discomfort surgical removal is sometimes advisable. The author usually soaks such a wound in hot water and then probes out the spines with a sterilized needle. It hurts but prevents one from limping around for days with imbedded spines.

Other Creatures—There are numerous other creatures that plague divers such as the lionfish, stonefish, sea snakes, jewfish, etc. They are common in cretain areas and deserve local attention. *Don't touch or disturb any animals or plants you can't identify.*

The creatures are one of the minor hazards of diving but they are a major element in the great adventure. The vital enemy in diving is *fear* which results in panic. Read and learn more about the creatures for it is their strangeness and your ignorance about them that ferment the crippling emotion of fear.

Plant Life—Other than the possibility of entanglement, plant life really isn't of any major concern for the diver. The giant kelp or seaweed areas of the ocean provide the possible places of hazard.

Actually, diving in kelp is an exciting experience but should be reserved for the veteran diver. This decision would be true of fresh water areas that have various plant growths of unusual lengths. The thin branches of kelp go from the bottom to the surface, where they form a canopy. In moving about under water, the diver often finds himself coming up under such a canopy. He should surface at the thinnest area, extending his hands overhead, parting the kelp to afford an opening for his head. The shortest route to open water should then be determined; the diver should submerge feet first and swim under the kelp, repeating this process until open water is reached.

The sports diver should always remain calm and think his way out of situations. If he becomes entangled in the kelp, he should slowly work out of it. Using force will only make the tangle worse.

DIVING PHYSICS

To fully understand the physics of diving the properties of certain gases should be known.

Oxygen—Oxygen is colorless, odorless, and tasteless. It occurs in a free state in the atmosphere of which it forms approximately 21 per cent by volume. Oxygen by itself is capable of supporting life and is used in some instances in lieu of air as a breathing medium.

Nitrogen—Nitrogen is the other main component of air. It also occurs in a free state in the atmosphere and comprises approximately 79 per cent by volume. This gas is odorless, colorless, and tasteless. In a free state it is inert, or chemically inactive, and as such is incapable of supporting life.

Carbon Dioxide—Carbon dioxide is colorless and has an acid taste and odor in high concentrations. It is a combination of two parts oxygen and one part carbon and is produced by burning organic material or by oxidation of food in the body. If the air supply is inadequate, or if breathed air is not properly exhausted or purified, the CO_2 concentration in the lungs will build up, causing panting and distress and finally suffocation.

Carbon Monoxide—Carbon monoxide is colorless, odorless, tasteless, and highly poisonous. CO is produced by oxidation of carbon-bearing materials when the oxygen supply is so insufficient that each molecule has only one atom of oxygen for one of carbon instead of two as CO_2. Carbon monoxide is found in dangerous concentrations in engine exhausts.

Components of Air—Normal Air (the atmosphere we breathe) is a simple mixture (not a chemical combination) of the gases described with traces of hydrogen and certain other rare gases. It is highly compressible. The proportions of the main constituents are approximately as follows:

	Per cent by volume
Nitrogen (approximately)	79
Oxygen	20.94
Carbon Dioxide	.03

Air has weight (1 Cu. PT. = .081) and occupies space. At sea level it exerts a force of approximately 14.7 pounds per square inch. This

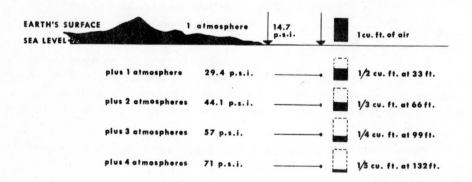

pressure is referred to as "Atmospheric Pressure." The word "atmosphere" is used to denote a pressure of 14.7 p.s.i. For example, the application of 29.4 p.s.i. pressure also can be expressed as applying a pressure of two atmospheres.

Basic Gas Laws—In addition to the properties of the foregoing gases described, the behavior of the gases is affected by varying conditions of pressure, volume, and temperature. There are several gas laws, which have been formulated and named for their originators, that describe the action of gases under these varying conditions.

Boyle's Law states that when a gas is subjected to compression and kept at a constant temperature, the product of the pressure and volume is a constant quantity, that is, the volume is inversely proportional to the pressure. *This is the most important law for divers to understand.*

Henry's Law states that the quantity of gas which goes into solution of any liquid is directly proportional to the partial pressure of the gas.

Dalton's Law states that the pressure exerted by a gas in a mixture of gases is equal to the pressure which that quantity of gas would exert were no other gases present.

Basic Laws Applied to Water—For practical purposes, the weight of fresh water is considered to be 62.4 pounds per cubic foot, and the weight of sea water is considered to be about 64 pounds per cubic foot. Since water is practically incompressible, the pressure which it exerts is proportional to its depth. For example, if a tank 33 feet deep is filled with sea water, the pressure which it exerts on the bottom will be about 2,112 pounds per square foot; this is equal to 14.7 p.s.i., or one atmosphere of pressure. This is the pressure exerted by the water alone; in addition the atmosphere above the water is exerting 14.7 p.s.i. also. The total pressure exerted on a body 33 feet deep in sea water thus is 29.4 p.s.i. Every foot in depth of sea water produces an additional pressure of 0.445 p.s.i.

Effect of Pressure on Gas Absorption—When water is heated, small bubbles can be seen rising to the surface. These bubbles are air which was absorbed by the water at low temperatures, its liberation illustrating the fact that heating a liquid decreases its capacity for holding gases in solution. Of special importance to the diver is the effect of pressure on gas absorption. Henry's law states that the solubility of a liquid at a given temperature is very nearly directly proportional to the partial pressure of that gas. That is, at two atmospheres of pressure, almost twice

What are the absolute pressures at the depths shown here?

How is the volume decreased at each depth?

How does this affect a diver and his air supply?

Evaluation Questions
WATER PRESSURE

as much gas can be dissolved in a liquid; at three atmospheres of pressure, almost three times as much; at five atmospheres, almost five times as much, and so on. It will be easily understood then that the decrease by one-half of the partial pressure of a gas absorbed in a liquid will liberate one-half of that gas from the solution. For example, carbon dioxide gas is absorbed in the liquid of a carbonated drink under several atmospheres of pressure; it is liberated rapidly in the forms of bubbles when the pressure is decreased by removing the cap from the bottle. The absorption by the blood and tiny tissues of nitrogen under considerable pressure is discussed under "Diving Physiology."

DIVING PHYSIOLOGY

Respiration—Man has a wonderful built-in system called respiration. It is this process that allows him to feed oxygen to all the cells of the body. The cells produce heat and energy with the oxygen and through the process of metabolism give off carbon dioxide.

The automatic action of the respiratory muscles move the chest wall, allowing the lungs to expand under the pressure of the atmosphere (14.7 p.s.i.). This air provides the oxygen which is carried by the arterial blood from the lungs and heart to the tissues. The venous blood in turn carries the dissolved carbon dioxide back to the lungs where it exchanges it for fresh oxygen.

Respiration involves an inspiration, rest, and expiration. This cycle is completed about 16 times per minute in an adult at rest. The average lungs hold about ten pints of air at full capacity. Normally they hold about 5 pints.

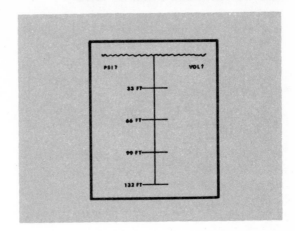

Diagram C:
WATER PRESSURE

Hard work will cause a person to breathe in about four pints of air beyond his normal one pint of expiration. He will in turn through forced exhalation be able to exhale about three pints beyond his normal one pint while at rest. The air that passes in forced inhalation is called complemental air; the passing air in forced exhalation is termed supplemental air.

The amount of air left in the lungs after the most forceful expiration amounts to about two to three pints and is known as residual air; therefore, in one deep respiratory exchange you can move about eight pints of air, but there is always a volume of residual air (two to three pints) left in the lungs. Recalling that air in the lungs or breathing apparatus displaces water, it can be shown how breathing can greatly change buoyancy. There is a twenty second circuit of blood as it carries the oxygen to the tissues and carbon dioxide away. The gas exchange in the lungs is called external respiration, while that in the tissues is called internal respiration.

Exercise causes a speeding up of all of these processes. The tissues demand more oxygen and produce more carbon dioxide. Certain brain cells are stimulated by this build up of CO_2 partial pressure; this results in a speeding up and deepening of respiration which provides more oxygen. The circulation is also stimulated and the blood diffuses more carbon dioxide into the lungs. The arterial blood leaving the lungs contains very little more carbon dioxide partial pressure than when a person is at rest.

There is much not known about what happens when the oxygen and carbon dioxide levels get out of balance. While the CO_2 level is the main

39

Where are the various air cavities of the body?

How is the used air exchanged for fresh?

What is the chemical mechanism that triggers respiration?

Evaluation Questions
RESPIRATION

regulator, O_2 plays some part in regulating emergency breathing. The body doesn't really set up an O_2 reserve nor does the blood have an unlimited capacity for transmitting oxygen when needed in heavy labor. An oxygen debt can be built up so that man can work beyond his maximum rate for a very short period of time; he consumes the oxygen later.

The body consumes oxygen on the basis of molecules rather than volume. At depth the air is compressed and molecules of O_2 increased. The air cylinder of SCUBA will be drained faster because the same volume of air must be maintained in order to purge the CO_2. The increased number of O_2 molecules therefore doesn't prolong the stay on the bottom; it becomes a surplus carried off with exhalation. Diving complicates the entire respiration process.

MECHANICAL EFFECTS OF PRESSURE ON THE AIR SPACES OF THE BODY-SQUEEZE

For discussion the effects of pressure on the body is divided into two sections. The first deals with the mechanical effects of pressure upon the body cells and spaces, the other with the physiological effects of gases diffusing into and out of the body fluids and tissues.

It is a remarkable phenomenon that the body can stand a pressure in excess of 2,000 feet without any apparent change, provided air has free access to all its surfaces which include the linings of the natural air spaces—lungs, middle ear spaces, and sinuses. The entire body (with the exception of any sealed air spaces) is made up entirely of fluids and solids which, according to physical laws, are considered incompressible.

Diagram D:
RESPIRATION

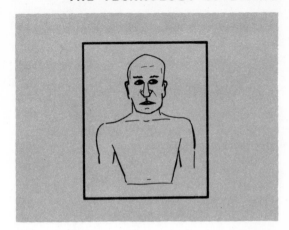

If, for any reason, air pressure is not applied equally upon all surfaces, (including the surfaces of the natural air spaces inside the body),

even a pressure difference of one-sixteenth of an atmosphere (about one pound per square inch) will alter the normal shape of tissue causing congestion, swelling within and bleeding from such tissue. These changes in turn cause symptoms of pain, shock, and cell destruction. The following paragraphs list the effects upon individual organs or tissues of the body.

The Lung—The effects of unequal air pressure on the lungs is illustrated by the skin diver who makes a dive by merely holding his breath. In this case the diver is subjected to an additional compressive force of one atmosphere for every 33 feet of descent. At a depth of 100 feet (as with pearl divers or record skin divers) the total pressure acting on his body amounts to about four atmospheres. At this depth, the amount of air which was present in the diver's chest on the surface, approximately twelve pints, is compressed to one-fourth its original amount, or three pints. This amount approximates the volume of the residual air of the lungs, normally the amount of air left in the lungs after the most

Which of the indicated depths relate to a limiting barrier to: closed circuit SCUBA, avoidance of decompression, avoidance of nitrogen narcosis?

Evaluation Questions
DEPTH BARRIERS

forceful expiration. The depth to which the unprotected diver can descend therefore is limited by the ratio of total lung volume to residual air volume. Should the diver now descend further, the additional pressure, unable to compress the chest walls or elevate the diaphragm further without injury, will bring about a condition known as a "squeeze." The effect of the "squeeze" is to force blood and tissue fluids into the lung air sacs and passages where the residual air is under less pressure than the tissues surrounding the chest.

The Sinuses and Teeth—In a similar manner, the membranous linings of the middle ear and sinus spaces are injured by a "squeeze" if the natural openings (ostia) of these spaces are blocked and do not permit equalization of pressure by free entrance of air. The prevalence of obstruction of the eustachian tubes is illustrated by the fact that at any given time 10 per cent of any group will have trouble adjusting themselves to rapid pressure changes for this reason, while about 1.5 per cent are affected by obstruction of the sinus passages. All sinuses are located within hollow spaces of the skull bones and are lined with the same type of membrane that covers the air passages of the nose. If pressure is applied to the body and the opening of any of these sinuses is obstructed by mucus or tissue growths, pain will be experienced in the respective areas.

With normal air pressure in the sinuses and excess pressure applied to the tissues surrounding these incompressible spaces, the same relative effect is produced as if a vacuum were created within these spaces. There is swelling of the lining membranes and, if severe enough, hemorrhage

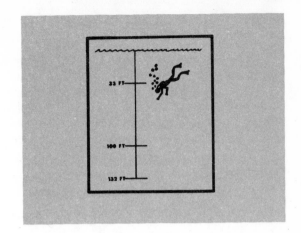

Diagram E:

DEPTH BARRIERS

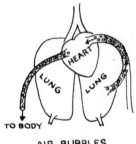

AIR BUBBLES
INTO BLOODSTREAM

into the sinus spaces will take place. This process represents an effort on the part of nature to balance the relative negative air pressure within the sinuses by partly displacing their air spaces with swollen tissue, fluid, and blood. A "squeeze" on the sinuses actually takes place.

AIR EMBOLISM AND RELATED ACCIDENTS ON ASCENT

Air embolism, one of the most serious and most frequent complications which can occur in diving, is caused by a relative excess of air pressure within the lungs. The conditions which bring about this accident are directly opposite to those which produce lung "squeeze." If a diver ascends holding his breath the air within the lungs will expand. Since there is no exit for this excess air, a pressure is built up within the lungs which is greater than the pressure surrounding the chest. This pressure overexpands the lung and ruptures its air sacs and blood vessels just as though they were partitions in an overinflated balloon. This can occur with only slight relative increases in pressure within the lungs, as during an ascent of only a few feet without relaxed respirations. Air is forced into these ruptured and torn blood vessels, causing bubbles to enter into the capillary beds of the lung. From there they are carried to the left chambers of the heart and into arterial blood vessels where they

43

produce the various symptoms of circulatory blockage in the heart, brain, spinal cord, or other vital organs.

Never Hold Your Breath When Using Scuba—Continue normal breathing during ascent. Air embolism can occur in six feet of water. The only indication of this overexpansion is a sensation of discomfort behind the breast bone and slight feeling of actual stretching of the lungs. Often there are no warning symptoms. Never ascend too fast. EXHALE ON YOUR WAY UP. The most dangerous area is 15' to 0'.

The extent of injury varies with the individual, the amount of air forced into circulation, and the length of time since the onset. Following are the symptoms in a severe type of air embolism.

1. A pulling sensation in the middle of the chest.
2. Reddish or other froth at the mouth.
3. Increasing numbness in the extremities, with arms and legs gradually becoming rigid.
4. Balance becoming unsteady; dizziness.
5. Convulsions and biting of the tongue.
6. Losing consciousness and cyanosis (bluish).

PHYSIOLOGICAL EFFECTS ON AIR SPACES

This section is concerned with the solution and dissolution of gases in the body tissues. These are often referred to as "indirect" effects of pressure and are mostly physiological in nature. The concern is not for ambient pressure and its variance with air spaces but with the partial pressures of the gases in the mixture a diver breathes.

Decompression Sickness—Nitrogen Absorption and Elimination—This phenomenon is called by many names, e.g., compressed air illness, the bends (pain in joints cause victim to "bend"), and caisson disease. It was a mystery disease for many years and even today there is yet much to be learned about the complete process as it affects different people.

What exactly is behind the illness? The common graphic simile is to take a bottle of coke and pry off the top. As would be expected, a charge of bubbles is released from the solution, pushes through the opening, and makes a mess on the table. These bubbles have been held in solu-

tion by the pressure but with the cap removed, the pressure is lowered and the liquid starts to bubble.

Whereas the bubbles in the coke were carbon dioxide, they are nitrogen gas in the diver's blood stream. Nitrogen (N_2) is an inert gas that serves as a bulk product in the air humans breathe. Under pressure it is highly soluble in the blood and readily absorbed into the tissues. N_2 must be released through expiration but unlike O_2 which is burned up by the tissues or CO_2 which is produced by the tissues, it cannot be released fast enough so it is absorbed. When the outside pressure is released, the N_2 must escape; if released too rapidly a state of supersaturation will exist.

Some supersaturation can be tolerated but at a certain point the N_2 gas will come out of solution and bubbles will form in the blood stream. These bubbles can cause circulation blockage in vital areas of the brain and spinal cord. Usually the bubbles will lodge in places of poor circulation such as the joints.

Some people are more susceptible than others to supersaturation. Older people, heavy drinkers, fatigued divers, and obese persons are far more likely to experience it. Fatty tissue has five times the absorption rate of water as normal tissue. Cold is another influencing factor on susceptibility. An individual may vary in susceptibility from time to time

The sensations of pain may come upon ascent for this is when the pressure is lessened and the nitrogen attempts to escape from the blood. Most of the cases occur, however, within the first hour the diver is out

of the water. Some cases don't show up until six hours later but rarely do any exceed twelve hours.

The *symptoms* usually center around pain in the joints, the leg joints more frequently than the arms. Pain in the muscles is also experienced. Other symptoms to be aware of are:

1. Dizziness (the staggers)—a good quick test is to have the diver stand with feet together and eyes closed.

45

2. Itching or burning of skin area. Skin tingling and numbness. Mottled skin (these are early signs).
3. Paralysis.
4. Shortness of breath.
5. Fatigue.
6. Unconsciousness.

The prevention of decompression sickness is the result of a planned dive. The guide for planning is the *decompression table,* a series of specified stops and at a rate of ascent calculated to see that the nitrogen pressure in the tissues never exceeds twice the pressure of the surrounding water. The bubbles will not form within this ratio of 2-1. Because of this the SCUBA diver who doesn't exceed a 33 foot depth can surface at any time regardless of exposure.

SCUBA divers should avoid decompression dives because of the limited air supply and the lack of recompression treatment chambers. Many things could go wrong—fatigue, a storm, equipment failure—to prevent the necessary stop of even a few minutes. Treatment is a long, painful, expensive process. It involves recompression under special treatment tables.

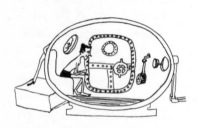

The best method of recompression is in a recompression chamber. If a diver attempts to recompress in the water with spare SCUBA, he should realize that improper treatment can leave him in a worse condition than if he had waited for proper treatment.

It is recommended that divers utilize the *no decompression tables* which follow:

COMPUTING DIVING TIME

The diver using SCUBA should remember that the total time consumed during the descent, and the time on the bottom, must be employed when using the decompression tables. The tables are calculated to include ascent time of 60 feet per minute, and this must be followed in order to stay within the tables. If the depth varies for any reason, and the deepest depth or longest time of any dive falls between the values given in the table, the next increment of depth or time must be used. The U.S. Navy has provided a repetitive dive table for dives within a 12 hour period. The table takes into consideration decompression on the surface between dives. It is a questionable recommendation for civilian divers.

	No Decompression Limits	
	Depth (feet)	Time (minutes)
60 foot	Above 33	No Limit
Rate	35	310
of	40	200
Ascent	50	100
only!	60	60
	70	50
	80	40
	90	30
	100	25
	110	20
	120	15
	130	10
	140	10
	150	
	to	
	190	5

Using the Table

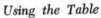

1. Allow a large margin of safety where-ever possible.
2. Hard work and cold water require an additional safety margin which must be figured.
3. Bottom time is descent time plus time at the bottom.
4. If your plans are obstructed or forgotten, stop at 10 feet as long as the air supply lasts. This is an emergency measure.
5. Prepare for possible decompression even when following a no-decompression plan.
6. Although a 30 foot dive of any duration requires no decompression, do not exceed the 60 foot per minute ascent speed.
7. A diver surfacing without making a stop should return immediately and repeat the stop twice.

AVOID DECOMPRESSION REQUIREMENTS IF AT ALL POSSIBLE! Use the no-decompression tables.

U. S. Navy Standard Air Decompression Table (1958)

DEPTH (ft)	BOTTOM TIME (mins)	TIME TO FIRST STOP	50	40	30	20	10	TOTAL ASCENT TIME	REPET. GROUP
40	200						0	0.7	•
	210	0.5					2	2.5	N
	230	0.5					7	7.5	N
	250	0.5					11	11.5	O
	270	0.5					15	15.5	O
	300	0.5					19	19.5	Z
50	100						0	0.8	•
	110	0.7					3	3.7	L
	120	0.7					5	5.7	M
	140	0.7					10	10.7	M
	160	0.7					21	21.7	N
	180	0.7					29	29.7	O
	200	0.7					35	35.7	O
	220	0.7					40	40.7	Z
	240	0.7					47	47.7	Z
60	60						0	1.0	•
	70	0.8					2	2.8	K
	80	0.8					7	7.8	L
	100	0.8					14	14.8	M
	120	0.8					26	26.8	N
	140	0.8					39	39.8	O
	160	0.8					48	48.8	Z
	180	0.8					56	56.8	Z
	200	0.6					69	70.6	Z
70	50						0	1.2	•
	60	1.0					8	9.0	K
	70	1.0					14	15.0	L
	80	1.0					18	19.0	M
	90	1.0					23	24.0	N
	100	1.0					33	34.0	N
	110	0.8				2	41	43.8	O
	120	0.8				4	47	51.8	O
	130	0.8				6	52	58.8	O
	140	0.8				8	56	64.8	Z
	150	0.8				9	61	70.8	Z
	160	0.8				13	72	85.8	Z
	170	0.8				19	79	98.8	Z
80	40						0	1.3	•
	50	1.2					10	11.2	K
	60	1.2					17	18.2	L
	70	1.2					23	24.2	M
	80	1.0				2	31	34.0	N
	90	1.0				7	39	47.0	N
	100	1.0				11	46	58.0	O
	110	1.0				13	53	67.0	O
	120	1.0				17	56	74.0	Z
	130	1.0				19	63	83.0	Z
	140	1.0				26	69	96.0	Z
	150	1.0				32	77	110.0	Z
90	30						0	1.5	•
	40	1.3					7	4.3	J
	50	1.3					18	19.3	L
	60	1.3					25	26.3	M
	70	1.2				7	30	38.2	N
	80	1.2				13	40	54.2	N
	90	1.2				18	48	67.2	O
	100	1.2				21	54	76.2	Z
	110	1.2				24	61	86.2	Z
	120	1.2				32	68	101.2	Z
	130	1.0			5	36	74	116.0	Z
100	25						0	1.7	•
	30	1.5					3	4.5	I
	40	1.5					15	16.5	K
	50	1.3				2	24	27.3	L
	60	1.3				9	28	38.3	N
	70	1.3				17	39	57.3	O
	80	1.3				23	48	72.3	O
	90	1.2			3	23	57	84.2	Z
	100	1.2			7	23	66	97.2	Z
	110	1.2			10	34	72	117.2	Z
	120	1.2			12	41	78	132.2	Z
110	20						0	1.8	•
	25	1.7					3	4.7	H
	30	1.7					7	8.7	J
	40	1.5				2	21	24.5	L
	50	1.5				8	26	35.5	M
	60	1.5				18	36	55.5	N
	70	1.3			1	23	48	73.3	O
	80	1.3			7	23	57	88.3	Z
	90	1.3			12	30	64	107.3	Z
	100	1.3			15	37	72	125.3	Z
120	15						0	2.0	•
	20	1.8					2	3.8	H
	25	1.8					6	7.8	I
	30	1.8					14	15.8	J
	40	1.7				5	25	31.7	L
	50	1.7				15	31	47.7	N
	60	1.5			2	22	45	70.5	O
	70	1.5			9	23	55	88.5	O
	80	1.5			15	27	63	106.5	Z
	90	1.5			19	37	74	131.5	Z
	100	1.5			23	45	80	149.5	Z
130	10						0	2.2	•
	15	2.0					1	3.0	F
	20	2.0					4	6.0	H
	25	2.0					10	12.0	J
	30	1.8				3	18	22.8	M
	40	1.8				10	25	36.8	N
	50	1.7			3	21	37	62.7	O
	60	1.7			9	23	52	85.7	Z
	70	1.7			16	24	61	102.7	Z
	80	1.5		3	19	35	72	130.5	Z
	90	1.5		8	19	45	80	153.5	Z
140	10						0	2.3	•
	15	2.2					2	4.2	G
	20	2.2					6	8.2	I
	25	2.0				2	14	18.0	J
	30	2.0				5	21	28.0	K
	40	1.8			2	16	26	45.8	N
	50	1.8			6	24	44	75.8	O
	60	1.8			16	23	56	96.8	Z
	70	1.7		4	19	32	68	124.7	Z
	80	1.7		10	23	41	79	154.7	Z
150	5						0	2.5	C
	10	2.3					1	3.3	E
	15	2.3					3	5.3	G
	20	2.2				2	7	11.2	H
	25	2.2				4	17	23.2	K
	30	2.2				8	24	34.2	L
	40	2.0			5	19	33	59.0	N
	50	2.0			12	23	51	88.0	O
	60	1.8		3	19	26	62	111.8	Z
	70	1.8		11	19	39	75	145.8	Z
	80	1.7	1	17	19	50	84	172.7	Z
160	5						0	2.7	D
	10	2.5					1	3.5	F
	15	2.3				1	4	7.3	H
	20	2.3				3	11	16.3	J
	25	2.3				7	20	29.3	K
	30	2.2			2	11	25	40.2	M
	40	2.2			7	23	39	71.2	N
	50	2.0		2	16	23	55	98.0	Z
	60	2.0		9	19	33	69	132.0	Z
	70	1.8	1	17	22	44	80	165.8	Z
170	5						0	2.8	D
	10	2.7					2	4.7	F
	15	2.5				2	5	9.5	H
	20	2.5				4	15	21.5	J
	25	2.3			2	7	23	34.3	L
	30	2.3			4	13	26	45.3	M
	40	2.2		1	10	23	45	81.2	O
	50	2.2		5	18	23	61	109.2	Z
	60	2-0	2	15	22	37	74	152.0	Z
	70	2.0	8	17	19	51	86	183.0	Z
180	5						0	3.0	D
	10	2.5					3	5.8	F
	15	2.7				3	8	11.7	H
	20	2.5			1	5	17	25.5	K
	25	2.5			3	10	24	39.5	L
	30	2.5			6	17	27	52.5	N
	40	2.3		3	14	23	50	92.3	O
	50	2.2	2	9	19	30	65	127.2	Z
	60	2.2	5	16	19	44	81	167.2	Z
190	5						0	3.2	D
	10	2.8					3	6.8	G
	15	2.8				4	7	13.8	I
	20	2.7			2	6	20	30.7	K
	25	2.7			5	11	25	43.7	M
	30	2.5		1	8	19	32	62.5	N
	40	2.5		8	14	23	55	102.5	O
	50	2.3	4	13	22	33	72	146.3	Z
	60	2.3	10	17	19	50	84	182.3	Z

Ascent Rate 60 ft. Per Minute

NITROGEN NARCOSIS

Popularly called "Rapture of the Deep" this illness is often not taken seriously. The novice diver should be assured that deaths have occurred as an indirect consequence of the actions of a diver so afflicted.

Nitrogen achieves high partial pressures at depths and the effect on the central nervous system is narcotic. It is similar to the reactions of someone given nitrous oxide (laughing gas) by a dentist in a tooth extraction. There are symptoms of confusion, loss of coordination, reasoning ability, sense of responsibility, sense of well-being, and false confidence. Reactions vary from person to person and within one individual from time to time.

The sports diver should never expose himself to this effect. It does not become an important factor until depths of over 100 feet are reached. Only highly trained and experienced persons should use SCUBA in these depths.

CARBON DIOXIDE TOXICITY

When the inspired air at normal atmospheric pressure contains 3 per cent carbon dioxide, the breathing begins to be noticeably increased; 6 per cent causes distress and 10 per cent or more, unconsciousness. Since 3 per cent carbon dioxide at surface pressure is about the maximum that can be tolerated without distress, it is essential that this percentage not be exceeded in the breathing device.

If, for instance, some carbon dioxide were allowed to accumulate in the breathing device, the result would be a higher percentage of carbon dioxide in the air breathed, and consequently this would increase the breathing rate. If more contaminated air is inspired, the efforts of the diver's increased breathing will be useless. Under such conditions, the diver will become exhausted not only from this labored breathing but from the toxic effects of carbon dioxide accumulated within the body tissues. Any attempt to work under such conditions will only aggravate the diver's condition because more carbon dioxide is produced by the exercise involved.

OXYGEN TOXICITY

Although oxygen is basic to life, an oversupply can produce certain harmful effects. At atmospheric pressure, 100 per cent oxygen can be breathed without harmful effects for periods up to 24 hours. Beyond this point, there are signs and symptoms of irritation, and accummulation of fluid in the lung. The safe concentration for continuous oxygen administra-

What diving illness do these symptoms indicate?

How could it have been prevented and how should it be treated?

Evaluation Questions
DIVING ILLNESS

tion over a period of days at surface pressure is about 60 per cent (as in hospitals, etc.).

The diver using pure oxygen is confronted with an additional danger caused by the increased pressure he encounters. Above 33 feet, high oxygen concentrations within the body cause strychnine-like effects upon the nervous system. Nausea, recurring periodically, is the symptom most frequently encountered. The most striking effect of oxygen poisoning at this depth is a convulsion which resembles an epileptic attack. There is a period of time before any of these symptoms occur. The time differs with the depth and the individual. Furthermore, the tolerance of the same individual on different days is highly variable and does not permit the setting of precise time limits for depths exceeding 30 feet. For this reason the *diver using pure oxygen for a breathing medium should not descend beyond 30 feet.*

With the exception of headache, drowsiness and laziness persisting for several hours following seizures, the symptoms rapidly disappear when

Diagram F:

DIVING ILLNESS

air is substituted for oxygen. The symptoms of oxygen poisoning, particularly the convulsion, are followed by apparently complete recovery.

The open circuit SCUBA diver need have no concern for oxygen poisoning as long as a normal mixture of compressed air is used. A depth of 10 atmospheres is required to produce dangers from the increase in partial pressure of O_2.

CARBON MONOXIDE TOXICITY

Carbon monoxide is one of the serious contaminants that sneaks into the breathing media. It happens when exhaust fumes from a gasoline engine get into the intake when filling tanks. It also happens when there is incomplete combustion of oil in an oil lubricated compressor.

Unconsciousness ensues without notice. Symptoms are cherry-red lips, face, and skin in contrast to the blue of anoxia. Use artificial respiration if breathing has stopped. Fresh air in itself will often be sufficient to revive a victim although an oxygen inhaler should be considered.

Language
and Lore of Diving

Every new activity develops its very own mysterious and colorful jargon. Skin and SCUBA diving has been especially prolific in this regard despite its relative youth as a significant sporting pursuit. Here is a representative listing.

Absolute Pressure—The addition of 14.7 pounds to the indicated gauge pressure. True pressure.

Anoxia—An insufficiency of oxygen.

Aqua Lung—A trade name now used interchangeably with "SCUBA" to describe the open-circuit self-contained underwater breathing apparatus.

Barotrauma—The direct physical effects of pressure changes.

Boyle's Law—The volume of a given quantity of gas whose temperature remains unchanged varies inversely with its absolute pressure.

Buddy Line—A line between two divers utilized to maintain communication, contact and position.

Buoyancy—The upward force exerted upon an immersed or floating body by a fluid.

Buoyant Ascent—Ascent utilizing an inflated life jacket with breathing apparatus.

Certify—To endorse authoritatively as being of standard quality, preparation, etc.

Chokes—A descriptive name for the symptoms of decompression sickness which involves shortness of breath and paroxysms of coughing.

Complemental Air—The volume of air which can still be inhaled at the completion of a normal tidal inspiration.

Compressed Air Demand Type Units—A breathing device using compressed air that is delivered to the diver through regulator unit, as he demands it by inhalation.

Compressor—An engine for providing a high pressure air supply in filling SCUBA cylinders.

Continental Shelf—The sea floor of less than 1,000 feet in depth which girdles the land masses.

Currents—Water that is running, moving, flowing, or passing—onward motion.

Cylinder—Used in diving to mean compressed air tanks.

Dalton's Law—In a mixture of gases the pressure exerted by one of those gases is the same as it would exert if it alone occupied the same volume.

Dead Space—The area of the respiratory system or the breathing apparatus wherein the last of every inspired breath is trapped.

Decompression—To release from pressure or compression.

Decrompression Tables—A method of computing decompression by stages.

Density—The quantity of anything per unit of volume or area.

Diaphragm—A dividing membrane or thin partition; that separating the cavity of the chest from that of the abdomen.

Dry Suit—A watertight rubber exposure suit.

Embolism—Air bubbles in the circulatory system.

Exhale—To breathe out.

Expiration—Act or process of emitting air from the lungs.

Gauge Pressure—Instrument indicating a change from normal atmospheric level.

Hemorrhage—Any discharge of blood from the blood vessels, caused by injury.

Hookah—The use of SCUBA but with the air supply delivered by a light hose from a surace source.

Hyperoxia—An excess of oxygen in the tissues.

Hyperventilation—The result of an increase in rate and/or depth of respiration over and above that required to meet the body's respiratory requirements.

Inhale—To breathe or draw into the lungs.

Inspiration—Act of breathing air into the lungs.

Kelp—Any of various large brown seaweeds.

Liberation—To release from restraint as in exhaling air from the lungs.

Apply Boyle's Law to this can of air at 33 feet. How much more air is needed to fill the can?

In what situations might the effects of Dalton's Law be of serious concern to a SCUBA diver?

Evaluation Questions
LAWS OF PHYSICS

Mae West—The standard life jacket used as an emergency safety device while diving.

Narcosis—A state of stupor or arrested activity.

Nausea—Any sickness of the stomach with a desire to vomit.

Nitrogen Narcosis—A state of euphoric depression resulting from increased partial pressure of nitrogen while diving to depths beyond 100 feet; narks (British); uglies (American); rapture of the deep (French).

Partial Pressure—The effect of a gas exerting its share of the total pressure in a given volume, such as oxygen or nitrogen in air.

Perforate—To pierce the surface of; pierced with a hole or holes.

Physics of Diving—The science of matter and motion.

Physiology of Diving—The organic processes and phenomena dealing with life; the study of the functions of the organs.

Recompression—The treatment of decompression sickness or air embolism in a recompression chamber using the treatment tables.

Reef—A chain of rocks or ridges of sand lying at or near the surface of the water.

Regulator—An automatic device for maintaining or adjusting the flow of air equal to the external pressure.

Rip Current—A body of water made rough by the meeting of opposite currents or tides.

Rupture—A breaking apart—burst, as an eardrum under pressure.

Sandbar—A body of sand built up by the action of the waves or current.

S.C.U.B.A.—Self-contained underwater breathing apparatus. Any unit that is free of surface functions taken underwater by a diver.

Diagram G:
LAWS OF PHYSICS

Skin Diving—Diving without the use of S.C.U.B.A.—Surface breath only.

Snorkel—A "J" shaped tube that is held in the mouth which permits breathing when the face plate is just under the surface.

Sports Diver—One who dives with or without S.C.U.B.A. for recreational purposes.

Squeeze—The decrease in volume of air internally and/or the increasing of external pressure often resulting in hemorrhage.

Staggrs—The symptomatic gait or walk resulting from decompression by stages.

Supplemental Air (expiratory reserve)—That volume of air which can be further exhaled at the completion of a normal tidal expiration.

Surf—Caused by the action of the waves as they break on the shore.

Surge—A great rolling swell of water. A violent rising or falling.

Symptoms—Any change in the body or its functions which indicates disease or accident.

Tanks—Also used to name compressed air cylinders.

Tidal Volume—The volume of air passing in and out of the lungs with each natural inspiration and expiration.

Toxic—Poisonous.

Valve—Any device that permits a flow in one direction only. A device that starts, stops, or regulates the flow of gas or air.

Vitality Capacity—The maximum volume of air which can be inhaled following complete exhalation.

Volume—A mass, often considerable quality; space measured by cubic units.

55

A Résumé of History

The tendency to think of diving as one of our modern sports is probably accurate but diving as a form of human activity has been engaged in since Biblical days. The sponge divers of Tunisia are still gainfully employed utilizing the same diving tools as those of ancient times—a loin cloth and a stone!

Homer's *Iliad* contains references to diving for oysters nad Herodotus (460 B.C.) speaks of Greek divers recovering treasure from sunken vessels.

Legends are recorded from all parts of the world that show that man by necessity has always harvested the sea from a point beneath the surface. Hunting, a major occupation of man until modern times, made the spearfisherman the leading participant in the field of diving until the middle of the twentieth century. The expert spearfisherman was a superb athlete who killed prize specimens to display and sell in the market place. Like all forms of hunting, however, spearfishing has evolved from a vocation to an avocation.

Man never has been content to kill an occasional beast; he must conquer and civilize the liquid jungle. It was so even with Alexander the Great in 356 B.C. who reportedly sat in an inverted bell in the water not to kill but to examine fish.

While a small group of fanatics hunted the seas, other individuals began a series of attempts to extend man's ability to stay under water. The early sixteenth century saw a man named Flavius Vegetius design a leather cowl with goggles of horn built in and connected to a skin bag on the surface filled with air. This was the start of an inventive and daring five hundred year period. In 1538, two Greeks in Toledo performed a "miracle" by staying submerged in an inverted bronze tub for approximately twenty minutes.

The idea of the diving bell seems basic to us now but the wisest men of the Middle Ages had trouble understanding the basic principle that the air inside the bell is pressed back by the water as it is lowered until its density equals the pressure of the water. Even Leonardo da Vinci failed to comprehend this necessity in designing a number of diving devices. The inventors kept at it, however, driven partly by the need to salvage pieces of artillery from the bottom of the sea.

Buonauito Lorini of Venice in 1609 devised a bell with a porthole and a long leather tube 30 feet long which fitted over a man to his waist. A Jesuit father and naval chaplain, Père Fourmier, wrote in 1643 of ships "that carried special officers whose duty was to dive into the sea to recover anything that may fall overboard." The idea of the bell evolved into a diving suit such as that of G. A. Borelli, an Italian physiologist, who suggested a goatskin outfit, tightly fitted, and attached to a metal container for the head. Borelli had the idea of circulating the air within and without this suit by means of a long brass tube—all the while "propelling oneself with flippers on hands and feet like the frog."

Physiology and physics, however, were the vital handmaidens to successful inventive genius. A sixteenth century record shows a breakthrough of understanding with M. Pascal's teaching of equilibrium of liquids wherein he explained that a compressible body must counteract the column of water pressing downward on it from above; that to breathe a man must inflate the lungs so as to raise this column of water. It was George Sinclair of Glasgow University in 1669 who explained the compression of air in a bell being submerged and the expansion upon ascent, thus showing that man is under uniform pressure as the water and air establish, by equal force, the necessary equilibrium. He also saw how air in a bell could be replenished through the breaking of emergency air vessels brought from the surface.

The seventeenth century was concerned chiefly with the diving bell although the Englishman John Lethbridge, a Frenchman Sieur Freminet and German K. H. Klingert individually improved the diving suit by introducing a bellow to pump air to the diver contained therein. British engineer John Smeaton gave the diving bell its final form in the late eighteenth century. He provided a circulation of air from the surface by means of a forcing pump and a tube; the excess air spilled under edges of the bell, and a nonreturn valve prevented air from being sucked out through the tube.

The history of diving has gone through stages as indicated by these items of equipment. What are they?

What inventor's name is closely associated with each item and what are the limitations of each?

Evaluation Questions

HISTORY

The nineteenth century brought about the reduction of the diving bell to that of a simple helmet. It was August Siebe in 1819 who designed the helmet, which was supplied with air from the surface by a pump, and unlike the present-day diving suit, was open at the lower edge. The Frenchman M. Cabirol joined Siebe in designing a cloth suit hermetically attached to the helmet. The French Navy adopted its use in 1860. About this time, two Frenchmen, Benoit Rouquayrol and Auguste Denayrouze, a mining engineer and a naval officer respectively, produced a "diving suit" with a metal canister of air on the diver's back. The air was kept under that pressure from above by a pump, but once a certain pressure of air was obtained the diver could detach the tube which connected him to the surface and become independent or self-contained. Most importantly, the outfit utilized a "regulator" which introduced the principle of automatically equalizing pressure between the water outside the diver's body and the air within. Jules Verne popularized this forerunner of SCUBA in *Twenty Thousand Leagues Under the Sea.*

Meanwhile, back in the laboratory, the physiologists were hard at work. As the inventors dared the deep with ever-increasing sophistication, the doctors began to explain what was previously not understood. It was the tragic results of "caisson" work, the use of a pressurized steel cylinder to keep water from in-water engineering work, that brought Frenchman Paul Bert forward in the latter part of the nineteenth century to explain the varying composition of gases in blood under varying pressures, the lucid and basic interpretation of decompression illness. His determination of prevention by slow decompression led to British physiologist J. B. S. Haldane's formulation of practical "tables" or rules for a progressive and

Diagram H:
HISTORY

therefore safe return to normal, establishing certain definite stages. In 1907, "Haldane's Table" was officially adopted by the Royal Navy.

The trend swung back to a form of diving bell with the advent of the twentieth century. The hunter still struggled in the water as he did in Biblical times, ignoring the new "devices" (Greek sponge divers destroyed the new-fangled apparatus whenever it appeared on their shores), while the inventor went ahead discovering ways to hunt and observe the sea life with more efficiency. The "chamber" idea, a bell with a closed bottom, now took over. An American (at last!) J. E. Williamson, a professional photographer, developed an efficient chamber of air to be used as an underwater motion picture studio. Then the American naturalist (note the new practical motivations behind the development), William Beebe and engineer Otis Barton descended with the Bathysphere to an ultimate depth record of 2,510 feet by 1934. The chamber was a suspended prison, however, and its passengers remained passive. In 1934 a Frenchman, Yves Le Prieur introduced a self-contained breathing device with a full face mask, with air suppled constantly at low pressure and used air escaping round the mask edge. The wasted air, however, required a manual regulating device and the inconvenience probably prevented Le Prieur's invention from becoming popular as sports equipment. Nevertheless, the French Navy adopted Le Prieur's apparatus in 1935; it introduced the following innovations: mask, gauge, harness, reducing valve, exhaust valve, and the breathing tube.

About 1938, a French Naval officer Jacques Yves Cousteau began to experiment with Le Prieur's apparatus. It was through an engineer, Emile

How are these sea creatures hazardous in diving?

How are they avoided and how handled if encountered?

Evaluation Questions
SEA CREATURES

Gagnan, that Cousteau derived the "demand regulator" principle which was in wartime use converting fuel for motor cars. In June, 1943, the man-fish idea was born as Jacques Cousteau went under with the modern aqua-lung; this was designed as a two stage air reducing valve system with the exhaust valve of air in the same place as the demand regulator.

What has happened since 1943? First, an extensive military concern with SCUBA diving to a point of renewed experimentation. This concentration provided a new breed of divers discharged into civilian life together with the surplus equipment left from the wars. These two developments spurred an economic market and commercial manufacturers entered the field to supply the popular growth of interest in skin and SCUBA diving. The physiologists had been at work while Cousteau initiated his SCUBA experimentation. American physiologist Albert Behnke, with a U.S. Navy team, was piecing together the puzzle of nitrogen narcosis, a limitation on both helmet-suit diving and SCUBA diving.

The Royal and U.S. Navies have led the research efforts in the past two decades in defining the medical aspects of both suit and SCUBA diving. The U.S. Navy's repetitive dive tables of 1960 have become a new milestone in the control of decompressors. Piccard's bathyscaphe has opened the era of the deep submersible with a seven mile dive; its versatility was shown in the search for the wrecked submarine, Thresher.

The sixties have brought us rapidly to a new point of concern. How can we free ourselves from the land and live indefinitely at any depth in the sea? In 1962, Hannes Deller, a new type of diving scientists, a Swiss mathematician, culminated a series of experiments with a self-contained

Diagram I:

SEA CREATURES

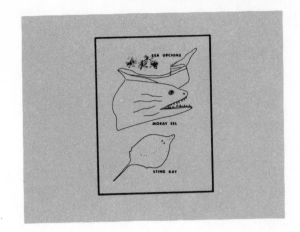

1,000 foot penetration of the ocean for a few short minutes. In 1964, George Bond of the U.S. Navy climaxed years of experiments with the conclusion that a diver reaches a point of supersaturation after 92 hours at a depth of 200 feet and no matter how long he remains under water, his decompression does not have to exceed 96 hours. He proved this with Sea Lab I, a laboratory on the bottom of the sea, where four men stayed at 200 feet for 11 days. Ed Link threw his inventive prowess and resources into a similar experiment and has placed men at 400 feet for several days (600 foot dives are now becoming daily routine for the new breed of "Life Support Scientists" of these research projects). Cousteau must not be forgotten, for he not only pioneered underwater habitation but also provided an example of modern comfort in group living under the Red Sea in 1963.

We are in a decade of exciting progress—the comet's tail of an extended history of trial and tragedy and growth. More than a sport, as you can see by the complex and serious development cycle, skin and SCUBA diving have been brought to their present state by pioneer inventors and scientists motivated in most instances by their own sporting natures.

Perhaps you are about to become one of the pioneers.

9

Rules of the Game

Diving doesn't have a set of competitive rules unless you're engaged in a specially organized activity such as spearfishing or photography. There are general rules, however, that should be followed if the journey under water is to be comfortable, safe and rewarding. There is no doubt that you would deviate frequently from such guidelines and emerge unscathed and well fulfilled but the stakes, often your life, are high in such a gamble.

Let's try a few of the frequent questions that cover the rules. You ask them and I'll answer.

1. *How good a swimmer must I be?*
   Ans: Watermanship, the ability (physical and mental) to be at ease in the water, is more important than swimming form or speed.

2. *How can I measure this watermanship?*
   Ans: A basic test given by the National Association of Underwater Instructors (NAUI) to candidate divers follows:

   A. Swim 200 yards without swim aids, demonstrating three basic strokes in the process (crawl, back crawl, back stroke, breast stroke, or butterfly).

   B. Swim 20 yards under water without swim aids. A diving start may be used.

   C. Tow an inert swimmer for 50 yards.

   D. Dive to 10 feet and recover a 10 pound weight or inert victim.

3. *What should my physical condition be?*
   Ans: Fit. Fit to match strength, endurance, and coordination against unknown environments, cold, and strange equipment. The Cureton

four-part fitness test available through the YMCA is a helpful measurement, or swimming a mile in open water is one of NAUI's ways to demonstrate your physical capacity.

4. *Should I look for bargains in equipment?*
Ans: You generally get whatever quality you pay for. There are bargains but you'll need to consult a veteran diver or underwater instructor before adding to your equipment.

5. *Do I need formal instruction?*
Ans: People have learned on their own and even from a book like this one. But life's too short for you to make all of the mistakes that are possible. Why not take advantage of a certified instructor who can expose you systematically to the problems and help you find the solutions without risking anything by trial and error?

6. *Can I dive if I have a sinus condition? How about heart trouble?*
Ans: Any physical impairment requires a doctor familiar with the medical aspects of diving to prescribe your limitations. Generally speaking, any sinus, nose, heart or lung difficulty places at least some, if not complete, restriction on you. But medical research is helping surmount such limitations. *Get a physical check up, whether or not you think you have an impairment.*

7. *Will I be able to dive in by myself while on vacation in the Bahamas this year?*
Ans: I suppose it could be a refreshing bit of solitude and adventure for you to stroll through an African jungle by yourself. The same problems come up in diving—the possibilities of injuring oneself, getting lost, overdoing—but these are somewhat avoidable by following the rule "Always Dive with a Buddy." However, choose wisely. A weak buddy is a liability to you and a superior buddy can push you beyond your limitations.

8. *Are spear guns easy to use? Am I lmited on what I can spear?*
Ans: There are many kinds of spears and spear guns, each and every one capable of dealing death to fish and diving partner. Always load or cock a spear in and under water. Keep a guard, e.g., rubber cork, over all points when not in pursuit of fish. Check local fish and game laws wherever you plan to dive. The fines and penalties for illegal infringement can dampen much diving enthusiasm.

9. *What is the red and white flag I see flying where divers are in the water?*
Ans: That's a diver's flag, a red square with a white diagonal running from the top of the hoist to the bottom of the flag. It should be

mounted three feet above the water surface wherever you are diving in order to warn passing boats to stay at least 100 feet away. Stiffen the flag with wire so it will not droop.

10. *How can I tell if the weather is good enough to go diving?*
Ans: Diving in rough or dirty water is considered foolhardy. Winds and white caps are a good indication of undesirable water; clarity can usually be determined by looking down from a cliff or boat. If diving in bad weather or rough water is unavoidable, then select an area with which you are very familiar.

11. *Do I have to be a skin diver before I start SCUBA?*
Ans: Many are not but the most effective SCUBA divers usually have been experienced skin divers. You shouldn't become dependent upon SCUBA or any equipment, for that matter, in deference to your own personal skills in the water. SCUBA diving is as easy as falling off a log but how far and what you fall into create hazards and complexities that are not always overcome by equipment alone.

12. *Should I practice breath-holding?*
Ans: Never while using SCUBA. It is necessary to respirate continuously in order to maintain pressure equilibrium. For this reason, always exhale upon ascending. However, knowledge of limitations, confidence, and extension of your breath-holding ability is possible through practice. Practice with someone watching you closely.

13. *How do I get new air for a SCUBA cylinder?*
Ans: Not from a gas station or a bicycle pump. It takes a specially filtered compressor or series of large supply cylinders operated by trained persons to do the job. You can usually get an indication of the quality and purity of the air by noting the housekeeping of the location, the location of the intake of the air, and the handling techniques of the attendant. If a wet fill is made, the cylinder is immersed to cool and prevent later shrinkage of air pressure.

14. *Should equipment be checked by a professional repairman even when apparently not defective?*
Ans: Yes. We recommend annual inspection and replacement of moving parts. Tanks have become of special concern and government regulations limit the period of use of a cylinder to five years unless hydrostatically recertified. Treat equipment like parts of your own body, and seek frequent examinations.

15. *How far down can I go with SCUBA?*
Ans: The answer is a question, why? Have a purpose for going to any depth beyond even one atmosphere or 33 feet. Anything beyond

132 feet means calculating decompression procedures during ascent. SCUBA for anything other than sport diving or in emergencies has capabilities to 300 foot depths, however, depending on the supply of air available. But don't dive deep for any records. Most of the daring record breakers are still on the bottom.

16. *How long can I stay down with SCUBA?*
Ans: This depends on your air supply again but no decompression tables should be your guide as a sport diver.

17. *How many dives can I make in a day?*
Ans: Each dive accumulates decompression problems, therefore repetitive tables should be learned to gauge the limits. If you have no tables, limit yourself to one dive beyond 100 feet in any 12-hour period. There is no substitute for a well-planned dive schedule.

18. *I forget so many things from one dive to the next that I've been making notes to refresh myself on places, creatures, and problems. Do others divers do this?*
Ans: We recommend a log book. It documents your experiences and provides vital clues to self-improvement as well as valuable information to science and other fields. The secret is to do the logging as soon as possible after a dive.

19. *What do I do if I see a shark?*
Ans: Respect its potential to cause injury as you would any other creature in the sea or on land which has the capability of doing damage. It's best to face such creatures, keeping within vision, and be prepared to ward it off if approached, with any object you can extend away from you. Hug the bottom if you are wearing SCUBA and work your way into shore or up the anchor chain to the boat.

Fear must be controlled to avoid any panicky activity on your part. The number of attacks by any kind of the billions of creatures in the sea is infinitesimal considering the millions of water exposures made by people annually.

Now You Are Diving

You should be at this point ready to conquer the last great frontier on the earth. With the basic introduction to diving presented in this booklet, and with a certificate of training in hand, you should be ready to fill your SCUBA cylinders and head for the beach. But what beach and with whom?

Divers are a gregarious lot and whenever two of them get together to swap fish stories, thoughts turn to a larger audience. The diving club is almost as much a part of the history of the sport as the basic equipment. Social interchange allows ideas to flow and joint efforts maybe made to apply the ideas. Remember, diving is a sport without spectators so you have to have to make the most out of topside diving contacts to get your full share of recognition and appreciation. You'll learn of new techniques, equipment and activities through club affiliation and you'll always be able to locate a buddy for a dive.

Diving clubs exist around the world and local chambers of commerce usually can direct you to your closest organization. The clubs have formed councils which guide the destiny of organized diving through the Board of Governors of the Underwater Society of America.

If you haven't gotten all of the training you want or you'd like to try being an instructor, there are two major organizations which sponsor extensive instructional programs.

The *YMCA* conducts a reputable program through its various autonomous branches following a set of nationally recognized standards. The *National Association of Underwater Instructors* is the professional organization of underwater instructors from around the world. It serves as the training arm of the Underwater Society of America and has headquarters at P.O. Box 54151, Los Angeles, California. NAUI, as it is called, is devoted exclusively to underwater education and its members train scientists, explorers, and sport divers in nearly every country of the world.

If America's number one hobby, photography, is yours as well, then you'll want to contact the Academy of Underwater Photographers at P.O. Box 54304, Los Angeles, California, and find out about membership, special seminars, the International Underwater Film Festival, and film programs near you.

Amateur science pursuits may be one of your interests and you'll find guidance for archaeology through the Council on Underwater Archaeology at 2647 Pierce Street, San Francisco, California, or marine biology or salt water aquariums through the American Littoral Society, Sandy Hook Marine Laboratory, Highlands, New Jersey, or exploration through the International Underwater Explorers Society, P.O. Box 233, Freeport, Grand Bahama Island, Bahamas. The Underwater Explorers Society has a headquarters at Freeport which features a complete country club and a research complex for divers.

You'll want to save up money and time as most divers are doing today and plan an expedition to one of the great new resort areas devoted to diving such as Bahamas, Tahiti, Hawaii, Mexico or one of the Greek Islands. This is the only way to experience the ultimate of all that diving can be, with 100 foot visibility, 80 degree temperatures and herds of wild creatures teeming over virgin reefs.

Whichever direction you head, whatever special interest you decide upon in diving, you'll want to read and keep on reading to improve your understanding and appreciation on every dive. There are many fine diving magazines put out by sea-oriented countries around the world but the American Pioneer, Skin Diver Magazine, will be your best regular contact with everything exciting that's happening in diving. Write SDM 5959 Hollywood Blvd., Hollywood, California.

If you need speakers or films to reinforce your group's diving interest, contact the foregoing organizations, diving equipment manufacturers, or your local sporting goods store. Meanwhile there's a treasure wreck on some distant reef awaiting you, there are award-winning pictures to be taken, a dolphin to play with, and a great adventure for every day left in your life. So what are you waiting for? Stop reading this booklet and start diving!